Summarization Across Languages, Genres and Sources (MultiLing 2019)

Varna, Bulgaria
6 September 2019

ISBN: 978-1-7138-0297-6

MultiLing 2019

SUMMARIZATION ACROSS LANGUAGES, GENRES AND SOURCES

Proceedings of the Workshop

September 6, 2019
Varna, Bulgaria

Proceedings of the Workshop MultiLing 2019:
Summarization Across Languages, Genres and Sources
associated with RANLP 2019
Varna, Bulgaria
6 September 2019

Designed and Printed by INCOMA Ltd.
Shoumen, BULGARIA

Introduction

Welcome to the MultiLing 2019 Workshop, collocated with RANLP 2019. MultiLing focuses on summarization, especially in tasks related to multi-linguality, different genres and sources, as elaborated below.

Summarization across languages, genres and sources: Summarization has been receiving increasing attention during the last years. This is mostly due to the increasing volume and redundancy of available online information but also due to the user created content. Recently, more and more interest arises for methods that will be able to function on a variety of languages and across different types of content and genres (news, social media, transcripts). This topic of research has been mapped to different community tasks, covering different genres and source types: Multilingual single-document summarization [Kubina et al., 2013,Gi annakopoulos et al., 2015]; news headline generation (new task in MultiLing 2019); financial narrative summarization (new task in MultiLing 2019, under a view of synergy and complementary to other workshops as in FNP 2018 at LREC'18 [El-Haj et al., 2018]); user-supplied comments summarization (OnForumS task [Kabadjov et al., 2015]); conversation transcripts summarization (see also [Favre et al., 2015]). The spectrum of the tasks covers many real settings, with varying intricacies, similarly to previous MultiLing endeavours [Giannakopoulos et al., 2011, Giannakopoulos, 2013, Elhadad et al., 2013, Giannakopoulos et al., 2015, Giannakopoulos et al., 2017].

Summary evaluation: Summary evaluation has been an open question for several years, even though there exist methods that correlate well to human judgment, when called upon to compare systems. In the multilingual setting, preliminary results have shown that several problems arise [Giannakopoulos et al., 2011], reducing the usefulness of pre-existing methods. The same challenges arise across different source types and genres, where different information needs are implied. We note that MultiLing also builds upon shared community tasks. This year these tasks concern headline generation, financial narrative summarization and summary evaluation. Based on previous experience, we estimate the number of participating systems to approximately 20 over all tasks.

Given the above, the content of the workshop includes: (a) selected system reports on the community tasks; (b) overview of the tasks and related findings; (c) selected papers within the MultiLing scope, but beyond the tasks themselves.

Organizers:

George Giannakopoulos - NCSR Demokritos (General Chair, Summary Evaluation Task)
John M. Conroy - IDA Center for Computing Sciences (Headline Generation Task)
Marina Litvak - Sami Shamoon College of Engineering (Headline Generation Task)
Peter Rankel - Elder Research Inc. (Headline Generation Task)
Mahmoud El-Haj - University of Lancaster (Financial Narrative Summarization Task)

Program Committee:

John M. Conroy - IDA Center for Computing Sciences
Marina Litvak - Sami Shamoon College of Engineering
Udo Kruschwitz - University of Essex
Horacio Saggion - Universitat Pompeu Fabra
Elena Lloret - University of Alicante
Vangelis Karkaletsis   NCSR Demokritos
Mark Last - Ben-Gurion University of the Negev
Natalia Vanetik - Sami Shamoon College of Engineering, Ben-Gurion University of the Negev
Josef Steinberger - University of West Bohemia
Laura Plaza - UNED
Florian Boudin - University of Nantes
Iraklis Varlamis - Harokopio University
George Petasis - NCSR Demokritos
Peter Rankel - Elder Research Inc.
George Giannakopoulos - NCSR Demokritos
Mahmoud El-Haj - Lancaster University
Ahmet Aker - Universität Duisburg-Essen
Giuseppe Riccardi - University of Trento
Corina Forascu - University "Al. I. Cuza" Iasi
Michalis Vazirgiannis - Ecole Polytechnique; Athens University of Economics and Business

Invited Speaker:

Horacio Saggion, Universitat Pompeu Fabra

Table of Contents

RANLP 2019 Multilingual Headline Generation Task Overview

Marina Litvak[1], John M. Conroy[2], and Peter A.Rankel[3]

[1]Shamoon College of Engineering, Beer Sheva, Israel

`marinal@ac.sce.ac.il`

[2]IDA/Center for Computing Sciences, 17100 Science Dr., Bowie, MD, USA

`conroy@super.org`

[3]Stratus Solutions Inc.

`rankel@math.umd.edu`

Abstract

The objective of the 2019 RANLP Multilingual Headline Generation (HG) Task is to explore some of the challenges highlighted by current state of the art approaches on creating informative headlines to news articles: non-descriptive headlines, out-of-domain training data, generating headlines from long documents which are not well represented by the head heuristic, and dealing with multilingual domain. This tasks makes available a large set of training data for headline generation and provides an evaluation methods for the task. Our data sets are drawn from Wikinews as well as Wikipedia. Participants were required to generate headlines for at least 3 languages, which were evaluated via automatic methods. A key aspect of the task is multilinguality. The task measures the performance of multilingual headline generation systems using the Wikipedia and Wikinews articles in multiple languages. The objective is to assess the performance of automatic headline generation techniques on text documents covering a diverse range of languages and topics outside the news domain.

1 Introduction

Headline Generation (HG) is an active area of research. A headline of a document can be defined as a short sentence that gives a reader a general idea about the main contents of the story it entitles. There have been many reported practical applications for headline generation (Colmenares et al., 2015; Buyukkokten et al., 2001; Linke-Ellis, 1999; De Kok, 2008; Gatti et al., 2016) or related tasks.

Automatic evaluation of automatically generated headlines is a highly important task, in its own right, where a candidate headline is assessed with respect to (1) readability (i.e. whether the headline is easy to understand), and (2) relevance (i.e. whether the headline reflects the main topic of an article).

The objective of the HG task is to stimulate research and assess the performance of automatic headline generation systems on documents covering a large range of sizes, languages, and topics. This report describes the task, how the datasets were created, the methods used to evaluate the submitted headlines, and the overall performance of each system.

2 Task and Datasets Description

The specific objective of each participant system of the task was to generate a headline/title for each document in one of two provided datasets, in at least three languages. No restrictions were placed on the languages that could be chosen. To remove any potential bias in the evaluation of generated headlines that are too small, the gold standard headline length in characters was provided for each test document and generated headlines were expected to be close to it. Two datasets were provided. Both are publicly available and can be downloaded from the MultiLing site.[1]

Wikipedia dataset

The dataset was created from the featured articles of Wikipedia, which are consists of over 13000 articles in over 40 languages. These articles are reviewed and voted upon by the community of Wikipedia editors who concur that they are the

---

[1]`http://multiling.iit.demokritos.gr/pages/view/1651/task-headline-generation`

1

Proceedings of the Multiling 2019 Workshop, co-located with the RANLP 2019 conference, pages 1–5
Varna, Bulgaria, September 6, 2019.
http://doi.org/10.26615/978-954-452-058-8_001

best and that the articles fulfill the Wikipedia's requirements in accuracy, neutrality, completeness, and style. As all featured article must have a summary, a subsets of these data were used at MulitLing 2013, 2015, and 2017 (Conroy et al., 2019). All the featured articles have titles for entire article and per section (sub-headings), thus, they also make an excellent corpus for research in headline generation. The Perl module Text::Corpus::Summaries::Wikipedia[2] is available and can be used to create an updated corpus. The testing dataset for this task was created from a subset of this corpus by requiring that each language has 30 articles and that the size of each article's body text be sufficiently large. A language was not select if the total number of remaining articles was less than 30.

Wikinews dataset

This dataset was created from the Wikinews articles. Since all featured articles have human-generated headlines, they make an excellent corpus for research in headline generation. The articles in this dataset do not have sub-headings, and only the main headline per article needed to be generated by participants in the provided test data. We manually assessed the collected data and filtered out files with small body or short and non informative headlines. The script for data collection is publicly available upon request. Table 1 shows the statistics about both datasets, including total number of documents, number of training and test documents per language, average document and headline length in characters (denoted by ADL and AHL, respectively).

3 Evaluation

3.1 Metrics

Both submissions were evaluated automatically, with help of the HEvAS system (Litvak et al., 2019). All headlines were evaluated in terms of multiple metrics, both from informativeness and readability perspectives. The informativeness metrics estimated the headlines quality at the lexical and semantic levels, by comparison to the content of gold standard headlines and the documents themselves.

The lexical-level informativeness metrics employed are ROUGE (Lin, 2004; Colmenares et al.,

---

2015) (ROUGE-1,2,SU,WSU) and averaged KL-Divergence (Huang, 2008). At the semantic level, we measured content overlap above abstract "topics" discovered by Latent Semantic Indexing (LSI) (Colmenares et al., 2015), Topic Modeling (TM) (Blei et al., 2003; Blei, 2012), and Word Embedding (WE) (Mikolov et al., 2013). The content overlap is calculated via comparison to the gold standard headlines (denoted by "similarity") and the document itself (denoted by "coverage").

The following readability metrics were computed: proper noun ratio (PNR) (Smith et al., 2012), noun ratio (NR) (Hancke et al., 2012), pronoun ratio (PR)(Štajner et al., 2012), Gunning fog index (Gunning, 1952), and average word length (AWL) (Rello et al., 2013).

The details about implementation of all these metrics can be found in (Litvak et al., 2019).

3.2 Baselines

For comparative evaluations and a possibility to get impression about relative performance of the evaluated systems, their scores were compared to five baselines that are implemented in HEvAS: (1) *First* compiles a headline from nine first words; (2) *Random* extracts nine first words from a random sentence; (3) *TF-IDF* selects nine top-rated words ranked by their $tf - idf$ scores; (4) *WTextRank* generates a headline from nine words extracted by the TextRank algorithm (Mihalcea and Tarau, 2004) for the keyword extraction; and (5) *STextRank* extracts nine first words from the top-ranked sentence by the TextRank approach for extractive summarization.

3.3 Participants

Two teams submitted the results for the HG task. The teams are denoted by BUPT (Beijing University of Posts and Telecommunications) and NCSR (National Centre for Scientific Research "Democritos"). Table 2 contains the details about each team.

3.4 Results

Figure 1 and Figure 2 show the evaluation results of informativeness for the generated headlines by BUPT and NCSR, respectively. Figure 3 and Figure 4 show the evaluation results of readability for the generated headlines by BUPT and NCSR, respectively. Based on the results, we can see that neither of submissions outperformed all baselines

---

Dataset	# documents	# languages	# training docs	# test docs	ADL	AHL	sub-titles
Wikipedia	9293	42	30–3793	30	32187.6	16.8	yes
Wikinews	3948	27	75–140	30	1450.8	40.7	no

Table 1: Dataset statistics.

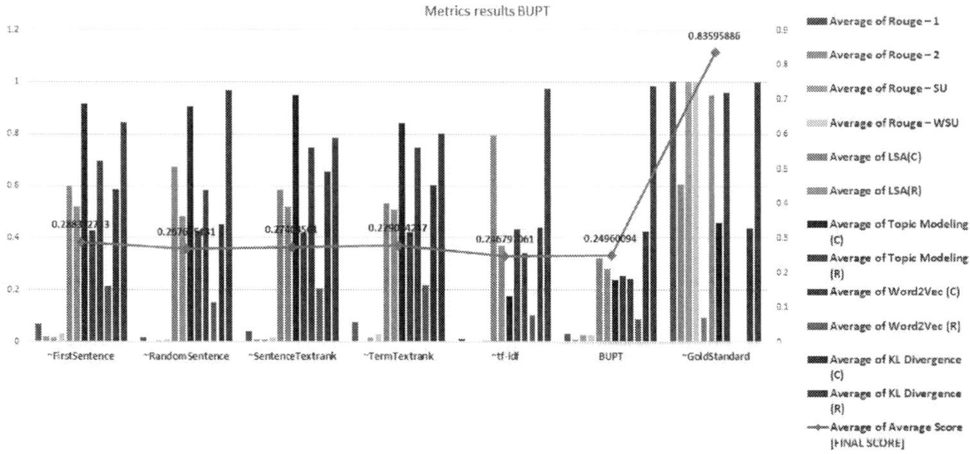

Figure 1: BUPT comparative results. Informativeness metrics.

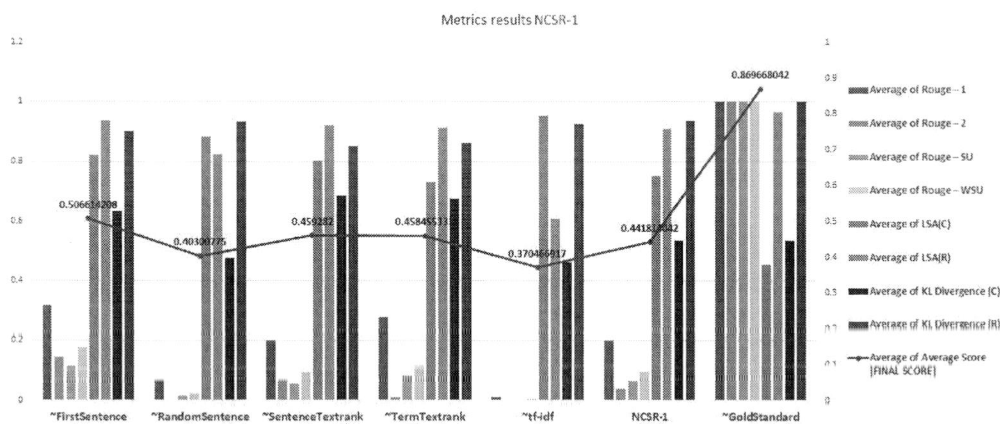

Figure 2: NCSR comparative results. Informativeness metrics.

Team	dataset	# languages	method
BUPT	Wikipedia	41	extractive
NCSR	Wikinews	3	abstractive

Table 2: Teams statistics.

in informativeness metrics. Because BUPT extracted entire sentences, their headlines are less informative but most readable. The NCSR headlines, conversely, are more informative than headlines produced by some baselines but not readable.

4 Conclusions

The Multilingual Headline Generation task presented the first open evaluation of multilingual headlines. Wikinews and the Wikipedia feature articles, both which have been used in previous multilingual summarization tasks proved again to be a great source of pre-marked data. In this first evaluation two teams submitted systems, one for each

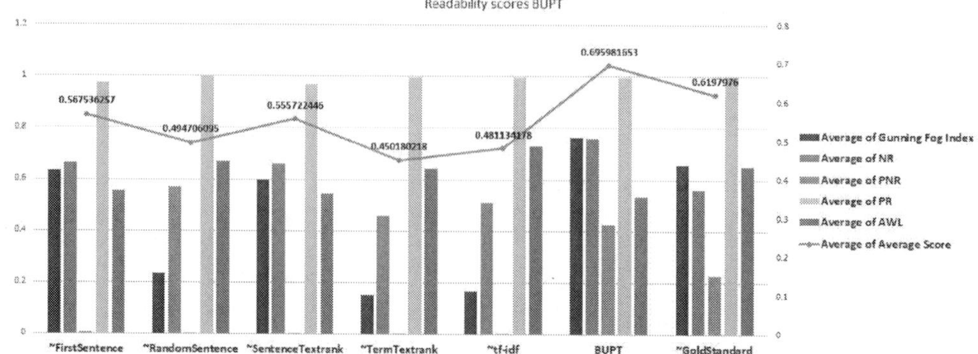

Figure 3: BUPT comparative results. Readability metrics.

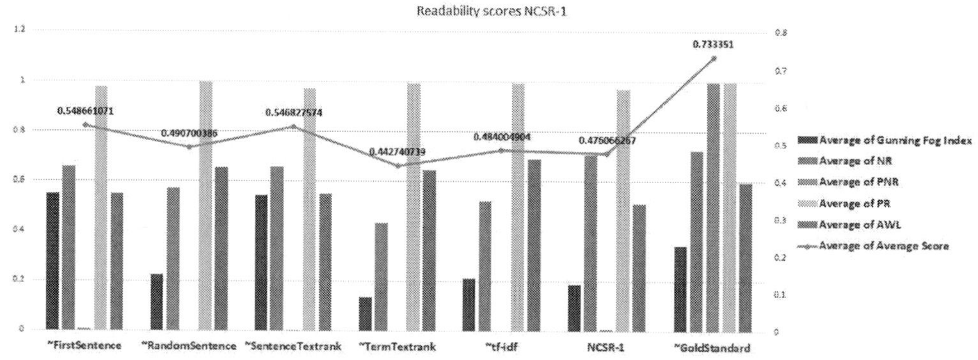

Figure 4: NCSR comparative results. Readability metrics.

task. Their systems were able to improve over some of the baselines. Further analysis of the submitted headlines, both system and baselines can be done to aid in development of stronger methods for automatic multilingual headline generation.

References

D M Blei. 2012. Probabilistic topic models. *Communications of the ACM* 55(4):77–84.

D. M. Blei, A. Y. Ng, and M. I. Jordan. 2003. Latent dirichlet allocation. *Journal of Machine Learning Research* 3:993–1022.

Orkut Buyukkokten, Hector Garcia-Molina, and Andreas Paepcke. 2001. Seeing the whole in parts: text summarization for web browsing on handheld devices. In *Proceedings of the 10th international conference on World Wide Web. ACM*.

Carlos A Colmenares, Marina Litvak, Amin Mantrach, and Fabrizio Silvestri. 2015. Heads: Headline generation as sequence prediction using an abstract feature-rich space. In *Proceedings of the 2015 Conference of the NAACL: HLT*. pages 133–142.

John M. Conroy, Jeff Kubina, Peter A. Rankel, and Julia S. Yang. 2019. *Multilingual Summarization and Evaluation Using Wikipedia Featured Articles*, chapter Chapter 9, pages 281–336.

D De Kok. 2008. Headline generation for dutch newspaper articles through transformation-based learning. *Master's thesis* .

Lorenzo Gatti, Gozde Ozbal, Marco Guerini, Oliviero Stock, and Carlo Strapparava. 2016. Heady-lines: A creative generator of newspaper headlines. In *Companion Publication of the 21st International Conference on Intelligent User Interfaces*. ACM, pages 79–83.

Robert Gunning. 1952. The technique of clear writing.
.

Julia Hancke, Sowmya Vajjala, and Detmar Meurers. 2012. Readability classification for german using lexical, syntactic, and morphological features. *Proceedings of COLING 2012* pages 1063–1080.

Anna Huang. 2008. Similarity measures for text document clustering. In *sixth New Zealand computer science research student conference (NZCSRSC2008)*. pages 49–56.

Chin-Yew Lin. 2004. Rouge: A package for automatic evaluation of summaries. In *Proceedings of the Text Summarization Branches Out workshop*.

N. Linke-Ellis. 1999. Closed captioning in america: Looking beyond compliance. In *Proceedings of the TAO Workshop on TV Closed Captions for the Hearing Impaired People, Tokyo, Japan*. pages 43–59.

Marina Litvak, Natalia Vanetik, and Itzhak Eretz Kdosha. 2019. Hevas: Headline evaluation and analysis system. In *Recent Advances in Natural Language Processing (RANLP)*.

Rada Mihalcea and Paul Tarau. 2004. Textrank: Bringing order into text. In *Proceedings of the EMNLP*.

Tomas Mikolov, Kai Chen, Greg Corrado, and Jeffrey Dean. 2013. Efficient estimation of word representations in vector space. *arXiv preprint arXiv:1301.3781* .

Luz Rello, Ricardo Baeza-Yates, Laura Dempere-Marco, and Horacio Saggion. 2013. Frequent words improve readability and short words improve understandability for people with dyslexia. In *IFIP Conference on Human-Computer Interaction*. Springer, pages 203–219.

Christian Smith, Henrik Danielsson, and Arne Jönsson. 2012. A good space: Lexical predictors in vector space evaluation. In *LREC 2012*. Citeseer, pages 2530–2535.

Sanja Štajner, Richard Evans, Constantin Orasan, and Ruslan Mitkov. 2012. What can readability measures really tell us about text complexity. In *Proceedings of workshop on natural language processing for improving textual accessibility*. Citeseer, pages 14–22.

MultiLing 2019: Financial Narrative Summarisation

Mahmoud El-Haj
School of Computing and Communications
Lancaster University
United Kingdom
m.el-haj@lancaster.ac.uk

Abstract

The Financial Narrative Summarisation task at MultiLing 2019 aims to demonstrate the value and challenges of applying automatic text summarisation to financial text written in English, usually referred to as financial narrative disclosures. The task dataset has been extracted from UK annual reports published in PDF file format. The participants were asked to provide structured summaries, based on real-world, publicly available financial annual reports of UK firms by extracting information from different key sections. Participants were asked to generate summaries that reflects the analysis and assessment of the financial trend of the business over the past year, as provided by annual reports. The evaluation of the summaries was performed using AutoSummENG and Rouge automatic metrics. This paper focuses mainly on the data creation process.

1 Introduction

Firms and businesses worldwide use a number of different methods to communicate with their shareholders and investors and to report to the financial markets. These include annual financial reports, quarterly reports, preliminary earnings announcements, conference calls and press releases (El-Haj et al., 2018a).

For the financial narrative summarisation task we focus on annual reports produced by UK firms listed on the London Stock Exchange (LSE). In the UK and elsewhere, annual report structure is much less rigid than those produced in the US, and companies produce glossy brochures with a much looser structure, and this makes automatic summarisation of narratives in UK annual reports a challenging task since the structure of those documents needs to be extracted first in order to summarise the narrative sections of the annual reports.

This can happen by detecting narrative sections that usually includes the management disclosures rather than the financial statements of the annual reports.

2 Related Work

The volume of available information is increasing sharply and therefore the study of NLP methods that automatically summarise content has grown rapidly into a major research area. At the conceptual level, text summarisation is the process of distilling content of a single document or a set of related documents down to the most important events presented in the correct sequence. Automatic text summarisation is therefore the process of producing a condensed version of a text using computerised methods. The aim is for the summary to convey the key contributions of the original text. Automated text summarisation therefore involves identifying key sentences. The process of defining key sentences is highly dependent on the summarisation method used.

The ongoing MultiLing series[1] tailored tasks towards multilingual single and multi-document summarisation aimed towards pushing the state of the art in automatic text summarisation and this year Multiling is introducing the first Financial Narrative Summarisation task focused towards English UK annual reports (Li et al., 2013; El-Haj et al., 2011; Elhadad et al., 2013; Giannakopoulos et al., 2011).

Cardinaels et al. (2018) is the only Accounting and Finance study of which we are aware that uses statistical and heuristic summarisers to generate summaries of financial disclosures. Results reveal that automatic algorithm-based summaries of earnings releases are generally less positively biased than management summaries, and that in-

---

[1] http://multiling.iit.demokritos.gr/

Proceedings of the Multiling 2019 Workshop, co-located with the RANLP 2019 conference, pages 6–10
Varna, Bulgaria, September 6, 2019.
http://doi.org/10.26615/978-954-452-058-8_002

vestors who receive an earnings release accompanied by an automatic summary arrive at more conservative valuation judgements.

de Oliveira et al. (2002) created a summarisation system that uses lexical cohesion[2] to summarise financial news collected from Reuters' Website[3].

3 Data Description

Before we indulge into describing the summaries dataset we start by a short introduction of what an annual report is. Firms in the UK and worldwide produce an annual document called an 'annual report' which provides a comprehensive reporting on a company's activities throughout the preceding year. Annual reports are intended to give shareholders and other interested parties information about the company's activities and financial performance. They may be considered as grey literature. It was not until legislation was enacted after the stock market crash in 1929 that the annual report became a regular component of corporate financial reporting. Typically, an annual report will contain the following (El-Haj et al., 2019b):

- Financial Highlights

- Letter to the Shareholders

- Narrative Text, Graphics and Photos

- Management's Discussion and Analysis

- Financial Statements

- Notes to Financial Statements

- Auditor's Report

- Summary Financial Data

- Corporate Information

Annual reports are usually long documents spanning between 60 and up to 300 pages. As the reports are provided in PDF file format, extracting

strcture is a challenging task. The work by (El-Haj et al., 2018b, 2019b) used the UK annual report's table of contents to retrieve the textual content (narratives) for each section listed in the table of contents. Section headings presented in the table of contents are used to partition retrieved content into the audited financial statements component of the report and the "front-end" narratives component, with the latter sub-classified further into a set of generic report elements including the Chairman's Statement, CEO Review, the Governance Statement, the Remuneration Report, and report's Highlights. Figure 1 shows a narrative example extracted from the Chairman's Statement Section in front-end of an annual report.

Chairman's Statement

Biocompatibles made good progress in 2004.

The Principal Investigators of the Company's PRECISION clinical trial presented positive data at the CIRSE' conference on 26 September 2004; and Abbott announced the start of a clinical trial for the evaluation of its ZoMaxx™ Drug Eluting Stent on 14 September 2004.

The Company is delivering its plan.

The Technology

Biocompatibles has a portfolio of granted patents around the two proprietary polymer systems – the PC Technology that formed the origin of the company and which is used by Abbott and Dideco, amongst other leading medical device companies; and the N-fil™ technology licensed from the Biocure affiliate of Novartis' Ciba Vision subsidiary and which is used in the Drug Eluting Bead programme. The patents provide a strong position over the use of these polymer systems in the target interventional products markets.

Figure 1: Front-End narratives example - Chairman's Statement

To detect the structure of UK annual reports we used the CFIE-FRSE software to detect structure for around 4000 UK annual reports for firms listed on LSE covering the period between 2002 and 2017 (El-Haj et al., 2014, 2019a,c; El Haj et al., 2018). CFIE-FRSE stands for Corporate Financial Information Environment (CFIE) -Final Re-

---

[2]Lexical cohesion refers to the way related words are chosen to link elements of a text. There are two forms: repetition and collocation. Repetition uses the same word, or synonyms, antonyms, etc. For example, "Which dress are you going to wear?" - "I will wear my green frock" uses the synonyms "dress" and "frock" for lexical cohesion. Collocation uses related words that typically go together or tend to repeat the same meaning. An example is the phrase "once upon a time".

[3]http://www.reuters.co.uk

port Structure Extractor (FRSE). The tool is available as a desktop application, which is freely available on GitHub[4]. The tool detects the structure of annual reports by detecting the key sections, their start and end pages in addition to the narrative contents.

Using CFIE-FRSE we divided the annual reports' full text into *training*, *testing* and *validation*. We also provide the sections extracted using CFIE-FRSE and we indicate which sections are the "narrative" sections, thus containing the textual contents of the annual reports (see Section 5 below for more details on how we define narrative sections).

For the creation of the financial narrative summarisation dataset we used a number of 3,863 annual reports. We randomly split the dataset into training (c75%), testing and validation (c25%). Table 1 shows the dataset details. We provided the participants with the training and validation datasets including the full text of each annual report along with the extracted sections and gold-standard summaries. At a later stage the participants were given the testing data. On average there are at least 2 gold-standard summaries for each annual report. We do not provide the PDF annual reports and instead we provide the full text as plain text file.

Table 1: Dataset

Data Type	Training	Testing	Validation	Total
Report full text	3,000	500	363	3,863
Report sections	60,794	12,089	9,247	82,130
Gold summaries	6,787	1,151	878	8,816

4 Task Description

In this task We introduce a new summarisation task which we call 'Sturece-based Summarisation'. In this task the summary requires extraction from different key sections found in the annual reports. Those sections are usually referred to as "narrative sections" or "front-end" sections and they usually contain textual information and reviews by the firm's management and board of directors. Sections containing financial statements in terms of tables and numbers are usually referred to as "back-end" sections and are not supposed to be part of the narrative summaries.

For the purpose of this task we ask the participants to produce one summary for each annual re-

port. The summary length should not exceed **1000** words. We advise that the summary is generated/extracted based on the narrative sections (see Section 5, therefore the participating summarisers need to be trained to detect narrative sections before creating the summaries.

Figure 2 shows the structure of the Financial Narrative Dataset. At the beginning of the shared task we provided the participants with two directories "training" and "validation" each containing the full text of the annual reports (*_full_text), the extracted sections (*_sections) and the gold standard summaries (*_gold_standards).

5 Data Sample

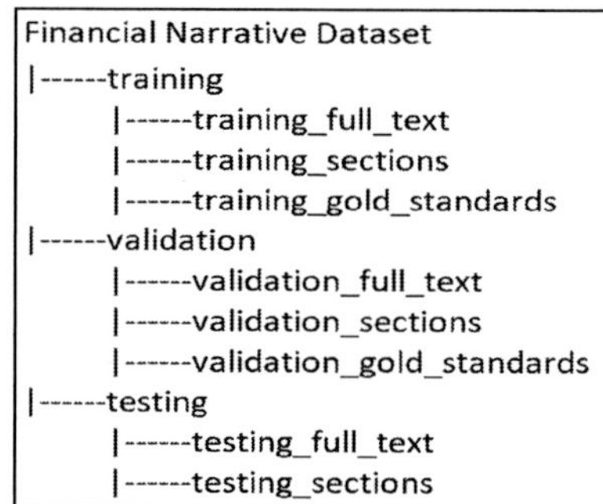

Figure 2: Dataset Structure

The data is provided in plain text file format in a directory structure as in Figure 2. Each annual report has a unique ID and it is used across in order to link annual reports' full text to their sections and gold-standards. For example: The *training* directory contains a file called **17.txt** where 17 is a unique ID and can be used to locate this report's sections in the *training_sections* directory, as shown in the files **17_896317_3.txt** and **17_896317_4.txt**. Also the same ID can be used to find this report's gold standard summaries as in the *training_gold_standards* as in the files **17_896311_8.txt** and **17_896313_1.txt**.

For the files in the *_sections* and *_gold_standards* each file name is made of the following: **reportID_sectionID_sectionType.txt** as in **17_896317_4.txt**.

Section type can be used to identify narrative sections, those with any *sectionType* but zero, as follows:

- 1 Chairman's statement

- 2 Chief Executive Officer (CEO) review

- 3 Governance statement

- 4 Remuneration report

- 5 Business review

- 6 Financial review

- 7 Operating review

- 8 Highlights

- 9 Auditors report

- 10 Risk management

- 11 Chairman's governance introduction

- 12 Corporate Social Responsibility (CSR) disclosures

Sections with *sectionType*=0 are considered to be non-narratives and are not expected to appear in the summary. Example: **17_896315_0.txt**. To make the task challenging we did not provide section types in the testing data as that is expected to be the participants task where they are expected to define which sections are narrative sections before summarising the report.

The data is available for free for research pruposes.[5]

6   Challenges

This is a challenging task considering a) the size of each annual reports and b) the lack of standardisation in UK annual reports. These challenges shed light on the complexity of financial narratives in general, along with the fact that more robust and up to date machine learning and NLP techniques are required to facilitate the automatic extraction and analysis of financial narratives.

7   Conclusion and Future Work

This paper introduces the first financial narrative summarisation dataset at the First MultiLing Financial Narrative Summarisation Task, held at MultiLing 2019 Summarisation workshop at RANLP 2019 in Varna, Bulgaria . It shows the need and as well as the challenges of summarising long and unstructured UK annual reports. For

the future work we will provide a baseline summariser reporting AutoSummENG and Rouge automatic metrics.

References

Eddy Cardinaels, Stephan Hollander, and Brian J White. 2018. Automatic summaries of earnings releases: Attributes and effects on investorsâ judgments. *Available at SSRN 2904384*.

Mahmoud El-Haj, Paulo Alves, Paul Rayson, Martin Walker, and Steven Young. 2019a. Retrieving, classifying and analysing narrative commentary in unstructured (glossy) annual reports published as pdf files. *Accounting and Business Research*, pages 1–29.

Mahmoud El-Haj, Udo Kruschwitz, and Chris Fox. 2011. University of essex at the tac 2011 multilingual summarisation pilot.

Mahmoud El-Haj, Paul Rayson, Paulo Alves, Carlos Herrero-Zorita, and Steven Young. 2019b. Multilingual financial narrative processing: Analysing annual reports in english, spanish and portuguese. *Multilingual Text Analysis: Challenges, Models, And Approaches*, page 441.

Mahmoud El-Haj, Paul Rayson, Paulo Alves, Carlos Herrero-Zorita, and Steven Young. 2019c. Multilingual financial narrative processing: Analysing annual reports in english, spanish and portuguese. *Multilingual Text Analysis: Challenges, Models, And Approaches*, page 441.

Mahmoud El-Haj, Paul Rayson, and Andrew Moore. 2018a. The first financial narrative processing workshop (fnp 2018). *LREC 2018*.

Mahmoud El-Haj, Paul Rayson, Steven Young, and Martin Walker. 2014. Detecting document structure in a very large corpus of uk financial reports.

Mahmoud El-Haj, Paul Edward Rayson, Paulo Alves, and Steven Eric Young. 2018b. Towards a multilingual financial narrative processing system. *LREC 2018*.

Mahmoud El Haj, Paul Edward Rayson, Paulo Alves, and Steven Eric Young. 2018. Towards a multilingual financial narrative processing system. *LREC 2018*.

---

[5]http://multiling.iit.demokritos.gr/pages/view/1648/task-financial-narrative-summarization

Michael Elhadad, Sabino Miranda-Jiménez, Josef Steinberger, and George Giannakopoulos. 2013. Multi-document multilingual summarization corpus preparation, part 2: Czech, hebrew and spanish. *MultiLing 2013*, page 13.

George Giannakopoulos, Mahmoud El-Haj, Benoit Favre, Marina Litvak, Josef Steinberger, and Vasudeva Varma. 2011. Tac 2011 multiling pilot overview.

Lei Li, Corina Forascu, Mahmoud El-Haj, and George Giannakopoulos. 2013. Multi-document multilingual summarization corpus preparation, part 1: Arabic, english, greek, chinese, romanian. In *Proceedings of the MultiLing 2013 Workshop on Multilingual Multi-document Summarization*, pages 1–12.

Paulo Cesar Fernandes de Oliveira, Khurshid Ahmad, and Lee Gillam. 2002. A financial news summarization system based on lexical cohesion. In *Proceedings of the International Conference on Terminology and Knowledge Engineering, Nancy, France*.

The Summary Evaluation Task in the MultiLing - RANLP 2019 Workshop

George Giannakopoulos
NCSR Demokritos, Greece
SciFY NPC, Greece
ggianna@iit.demokritos.gr

Nikiforos Pittaras
NCSR Demokritos, Greece
DIT, NKUA
pittarasnikif@iit.demokritos.gr

Abstract

This report covers the summarization evaluation task, proposed to the summarization community via the MultiLing 2019 Workshop of the RANLP 2019 conference. The task aims to encourage the development of automatic summarization evaluation methods closely aligned with manual, human-authored summary grades and judgements. A multilingual setting is adopted, building upon a corpus of Wikinews articles across 6 languages (English, Arabic, Romanian, Greek, Spanish and Czech). The evaluation utilizes human (golden) and machine-generated (peer) summaries, which have been assigned human evaluation scores from previous MultiLing tasks. Using these resources, the original corpus is augmented with synthetic data, combining summary texts under three different strategies (`reorder`, `merge` and `replace`), each engineered to introduce noise in the summary in a controlled and quantifiable way. We estimate that the utilization of such data can extract and highlight useful attributes of summary quality estimation, aiding the creation of data-driven automatic methods with an increased correlation to human summary evaluations across domains and languages. This paper provides a brief description of the summary evaluation task, the data generation protocol and the resources made available by the MultiLing community, towards improving automatic summarization evaluation.

1 Introduction and motivation

Automatic summary evaluation is related to the problem of how to automatically evaluate a summary of a larger source text. A body of work has produced popular methods, which build upon and rely on a small set human-authored summaries (often dubbed "golden" or "model" summaries) to be able to judge machine-generated summaries in an automated manner (e.g., (Lin, 2004; Hovy et al., 2005)). Additionally, there exists related work on fully automatic evaluation of summaries, without the need of model summaries (Louis and Nenkova, 2012; Saggion et al., 2010).

However, summary evaluation has remained an open problem in the summarization community for several years. Despite some progress in the engineered evaluation measures in producing results with an acceptable correlation with human judgements (Lin, 2004; Giannakopoulos et al., 2017; Giannakopoulos, 2009), application of these approaches in (a) multiple languages, and (b) multiple domains, illustrates that they may exhibit low robustness and consistency across these variable settings (Giannakopoulos et al., 2011). These pitfalls come to complement a set of other challenges that have been identified in the related literature, such as the usefulness in different variations of established methods (Rankel et al., 2013), the negligence over different components of human evaluation (Graham, 2015), the dangers of combining measures (Conroy and Dang, 2008), etc.

Given this set of issues, we extend previous work on summarization evaluation, including and focusing on the effect of sentence order on summary evaluation scores (Madnani et al., 2007). To this end, in this task we provide dataset resources rich with reordered sum-

Proceedings of the Multiling 2019 Workshop, co-located with the RANLP 2019 conference, pages 11–16
Varna, Bulgaria, September 6, 2019.
http://doi.org/10.26615/978-954-452-058-8_003

mary instances, ranging from single to multi-sentence shuffles and sentence swaps across summaries. Finally, our contribution adopts a multi-lingual setting, going beyond English summary data and including languages with far less resources in the NLP and summarization research community. We describe these contributions in detail, starting with the introduction of the summary evaluation task in Section 2, followed by a description of the data generation process in Section 3. We conclude with a discussion on the utility of the provided summary resources (Section 4) and conclude with an outline of this paper, along with future work and next steps of the MultiLing community.

2 The Summary Evaluation Task

Given the aforementioned issues and building on previous work of the MultiLing community as well as past efforts undertaken in previous MultiLing workshops, this year we relaunch the MultiLing Summary Evaluation task within and beyond the 2019 workshop. In the next paragraphs, we define the task, elaborate on the accompanying data and describe the evaluation methodology and utility of the provided resources.

2.1 Problem definition and scope

The summary evaluation tasks aims to incentivize the construction of automatic summary evaluation systems that produce judgements that correlate highly with corresponding feedback from human evaluators. As previously elaborated, such systems should wield desirable properties that go beyond existing work in summary evaluation methods, i.e.:

- Display a degree of robustness against multilingual application, being able to produce qualitative evaluations on a range of input languages.

- Be applicable in more than one domain. This trait could manifest itself as a language-agnostic pipeline, the application of transfer learning and domain adaptation, etc.

To aid the construction of such systems, we provide a collection of resources along with the support and expertise of the Multi-Ling community. Specifically, as part of the MultiLing2019 effort, we have generated and made publicly available a diverse multilingual dataset (as well as a collection of tools, services and web infrastructure, expected to be finalized within the year) described in the following sections.

3 A Synthetic Summary Evaluation Dataset

Continuing from the 2017 workshop, we have renewed the data generation architecture and methodology, paired with an updated infrastructure support roadmap for the task.

3.1 Source data

We utilize compiled datasets from previous MultiLing tasks (Giannakopoulos et al., 2011; Kubina et al., 2013; Giannakopoulos et al., 2015; Giannakopoulos et al., 2017), composed of multilingual news articles from Wikinews[1]. Each article is paired with model ("golden") summaries, as well as graded, machine-generated summaries from past MultiLing participants. Specifically, we use the source documents and golden summaries of the MultiLing 2013 multilingual and multi-document summarization task. The data consists of a collection of 15 topics with source articles for a number languages. We select languages with coverage over the entirety of the topics, arriving at a total of 6 languages with approximately 5 source articles each, i.e. Arabic, Czech, English, Greek, Romanian, Spanish.

Additionally, we utilize the automatic summaries generated by participant systems in the workshop of that year (Kubina et al., 2013; Giannakopoulos, 2013) along with human-annotated grades. The total number of files (summaries and full source texts) per language are listed in Table 1.

3.2 Synthetic Data Generation

Using the dataset described above, we apply data augmentation methods to produce additional summaries, via an application of an array of summary transformation or "scrambling" mechanisms. The purpose of these op-

[1] https://en.wikinews.org/wiki/Main_Page

	Original input dataset					
split	train			test		
language	sources	models	peers - scores	sources	models	peers - scores
Arabic	75	60	150	75	30	75
Czech	75	60	90	75	30	45
English	75	60	148	75	30	74
Greek	75	60	90	75	30	45
Romanian	75	60	90	75	30	45
Spanish	75	60	90	75	30	45

Table 1: Total number of train / test set source documents, model summaries and evaluated peer summaries, per language in the summary evaluation task input dataset, across all 15 document topics.

	Original input dataset					
split	train			test		
type	sources	models	peers - scores	sources	models	peers - scores
count	450	180	329	450	90	390
	Synthetic dataset					
split	train			test		
type	sources	models	peers - scores	sources	models	peers - scores
count	N/A	6300	11515	N/A	3150	13650

Table 2: Total source documents, model and evaluated peer summaries, for all languages and topics. We provide the counts for (a) the original MultiLing summary and source data in the input dataset (top), (b) the total data produced by processing the input via the synthetic generation process (bottom), for each input summary type.

erators are to introduce noise in a systematic manner, with the amount of such disturbances affecting the original summary quality in a predictable way. Each such process utilizes input summary data to produce a new synthetic summary, by introducing randomness at the sentence level. The input to this process is either a single summary or a combination of multiple summaries, as outlined in the method descriptions below:

1. **Sentence reordering (SO)**: this method operates at the level of a single summary. Given an input summary S in the form of a collection of sentences s_i, $S = \{s_1, s_2, \ldots, s_N\}$, SO scrambling produces an output summary $F_{SO}(S)$, where $F()$ is a random shuffle operation assuming the form of a derangement (de Montmort, 1713) – i.e. identity mappings of the source elements are avoided. Evaluation on output data from this strategy should capture the impact of sentence order in summary evaluation methods.

2. **Sentence replacement (SR)**: here, the output summary is produced by two steps of random selection. First, a number of sentences $s_i \in S$ are randomly chosen from the input summary to be replaced. Subsequently, replacement sentences are randomly picked from other summary files, which is implemented as follows. First, all available tuples (S_r, s_j) are generated, with S_r denoting other summaries (different than S) in the available pool for the same topic and language as S, and s_j a sentence in S_r. We then randomly select one replacement tuple for each input sentence marked for replacement, swapping the latter with the corresponding summary / sentence source contained in the tuple. This strategy extends upon SO by also considering content scrambling across different summaries, along sentence order within the input summary; this is meant to identify how overall quality of the constituent

Composite Dataset, v1							
split	train				test		
type	sources	models	peers - scores	synth	sources	models	peers - scores	synth
count	450	180	329	0	450	90	390	1890
Composite Dataset, v2							
split	train				test		
type	sources	models	peers - scores	synth	sources	models	peers - scores	synth
count	450	180	329	17815	450	90	390	16800

Table 3: Total source documents, model summaries, evaluated peer summaries and synthetic summaries, for all languages and topics in the provided dataset versions. The current version of the composite dataset (v1, top) includes a subset of the synthetic data in the test portion of the dataset. Version v2 (bottom) contains the entirety of the generated synthetic data.

summaries tends to influence the resulting mixed summary.

3. **Summary merging (ME)**: The merging scrambling method is the final operator examined in our approach, and is a coarse-grained version of SR. Here, the scrambling does not operate on the sentence level, but splits the entire summary into two halves. The split is computed with respect to number sentences, not characters, i.e. $S_{first} = \{s_i \in S : i \leq |S|/2\}$ and $S_{second} = \{s_i \in S : i > |S|/2\}$ where $|S|$ denotes the sentence set cardinality for the summary. One of the two halves is subsequently randomly selected to be replaced with a corresponding half (e.g. a first (second) half is only replaced with another first (second) half) from another randomly selected summary for the same topic and language. This approach extends on SO and SR by introducing a potential change in the overall length of the summary, along with random replacement of summary content.

Having these scrambling options, we generate 5 randomized samples per strategy and summary file of the compiled input dataset described above. For each of the 5 samples, how each scrambling strategy is applied (e.g. which sentences are reordered in SO and how, which replacement summaries are selected in SR and ME, and so on) is randomly decided, leading to variations between them. Additionally, for the modification strategies that operate on the sentence level (i.e. SO and SR), we vary the percentage p of the sentences affected,

$p \in \{20, 40, 60\}$. For example, for $p = 20$, approximately 20% of the summary sentences are randomly reordered in SO scrambling, while 20% of source sentences are replaced when SR scrambling is applied. The percentage determines the amount of scrambling noise the post-processing step introduces, which is expected to be associated with a corresponding change in quality in the synthetic output summary.

3.3 Available datasets

The two configuration modifiers (i.e. the amount of noise and number of repetitions) combined with the three strategies described above, result in the generation of 35 synthetic samples, for each summary in the original input dataset. The total number of synthetic data generated is detailed in table 2 and compared with the counts of the original assembled source data described in Section 3.1. The augmentation process results in a well-populated collection of summaries; we estimate that this volume of data will be able to leverage and support a productive and fruitful summary evaluation task.

In the following weeks, the MultiLing community will launch a large-scale human evaluation effort in order to annotate the synthetic summaries with manual evaluation scores. Until the completion of this task, we provide two dataset versions to the summarization community. These datasets are illustrated in Table 3. The compacted version (v1) consists of the original source data, with the test set extended with a small, representative sample of the synthetic data. This sample is extracted by including 3 random representatives for each scrambling strategy and noise strength for each topic / language pair, resulting in a total of $6 \times 15 \times (2 \times 3 + 1) \times 3 = 1890$ synthetic summaries for the test set. We do not extend the training portion, given the lack of human evaluation scores for the synthetic data. However, we provide the full composite dataset to interested parties, amounting to a total of 17815 and 16800 synthetic summaries, for the train and test portion of the dataset, respectively. Both dataset versions are publicly available in the MultiLing community website [2].

3.4 Implementation

We used Python v3.7 to generate the synthetic summaries. Language-aware sentence splitting was performed using the Stanford CoreNLP library[3](Manning et al., 2014), along with the pycountry[4] library for locale processing. The NLTK [5] (Loper and Bird, 2002) package was used for generic text processing and manipulation tasks.

3.5 Evaluation plan

As mentioned previously, the manual evaluation of the synthetic data is currently in progress, utilizing resources and expertise within the MultiLing community. The available datasets will be incrementally updated with evaluation scores, as the latter are being aggregated and incorporated. Additionally, in the immediate future, MultiLing will further support the summary evaluation task by introducing an automatic evaluation platform on the MultiLing website [6], along with an array of usability, user experience and interface improvements to the community webpage. Further, we will examine providing means and support for crowd-sourcing (Pittaras et al., 2019), to aid and reduce the cost of human evaluation in summarization tasks.

4 Discussion

The generated dataset provides summaries of variable quality, spread across multiple, iden-tifiable noise categories (e.g. sentence order, sentence replacement and merging). We expect this engineered feature to aid the development of evaluation approaches and measures that attempt to capture and highlight such artifacts, as an additional stepping stone to arriving at high correlation to human judgements. Specifically, we emphasize the importance of detection and quantification of the degree of alignment of such automatic evaluations and human grades. This alignment should capture, encapsulate and be influenced by details of the synthetic generation process of a summary (i.e. which scrambling method is applied), the amount of noise introduced (e.g. number and distance of reordered sentences), the evaluated quality of the source summary / summaries (e.g. a combination of the grades of two merged summary parts), etc. Finally, additional avenues for alignment to human scores (e.g. degrees of qualitative deviation, corresponding to the aforementioned factors) could be discovered on top of the provided ones, via engineered or automatic methods.

5 Future work and conclusions

In this paper we have provided a brief description of the summary evaluation task, bootstrapped in the MultiLing 2019 workshop. We have described in detail a synthetic data generation process, making publicly available two versions of a composite dataset (containing synthetic and non-synthetic data) that is produced from it. We believe that these data can be utilized towards generating efficient and robust summary evaluation approaches.

Within the next months, we will work on the human evaluation task of the generated synthetic data. Additionally, we will implement the evaluation steps outlined in Section 3.5, in order to create an accessible benchmark towards incentivizing the improvement automatic summary evaluation methods. Furthermore, we will make available a corresponding augmented dataset using domains different from news articles, utilizing MultiLing corpora from other workshop tasks. Additionally, appropriate dissemination and outreach steps will be taken to further encourage participation in the summary evaluation task within and beyond the MultiLing community.

References

John M. Conroy and Hoa Trang Dang. 2008. Mind the gap: Dangers of divorcing evaluations of summary content from linguistic quality. In *Proceedings of the 22nd International Conference on Computational Linguistics (Coling 2008)*, pages 145–152, Manchester, UK, August. Coling 2008 Organizing Committee.

Pierre Rémond de Montmort. 1713. *Essay d'analyse sur les jeux de hazard.* C. Jombert.

George Giannakopoulos, Mahmoud El-Haj, Benoit Favre, Marina Litvak, Josef Steinberger, and Vasudeva Varma. 2011. Tac 2011 multiling pilot overview.

George Giannakopoulos, Jeff Kubina, John Conroy, Josef Steinberger, Benoit Favre, Mijail Kabadjov, Udo Kruschwitz, and Massimo Poesio. 2015. Multiling 2015: multilingual summarization of single and multi-documents, on-line fora, and call-center conversations. In *Proceedings of the 16th Annual Meeting of the Special Interest Group on Discourse and Dialogue*, pages 270–274.

George Giannakopoulos, John Conroy, Jeff Kubina, Peter A Rankel, Elena Lloret, Josef Steinberger, Marina Litvak, and Benoit Favre. 2017. Multiling 2017 overview. In *Proceedings of the MultiLing 2017 workshop on summarization and summary evaluation across source types and genres*, pages 1–6.

George Giannakopoulos. 2009. Automatic summarization from multiple documents. *Ph. D. dissertation.*

George Giannakopoulos. 2013. Multi-document multilingual summarization and evaluation tracks in acl 2013 multiling workshop. In *Proceedings of the MultiLing 2013 Workshop on Multilingual Multi-document Summarization*, pages 20–28.

Yvette Graham. 2015. Re-evaluating automatic summarization with BLEU and 192 shades of ROUGE. In *Proceedings of the 2015 Conference on Empirical Methods in Natural Language Processing*, pages 128–137, Lisbon, Portugal, September. Association for Computational Linguistics.

E. Hovy, C. Y. Lin, L. Zhou, and J. Fukumoto. 2005. Basic elements.

Jeff Kubina, John Conroy, and Judith Schlesinger. 2013. Acl 2013 multiling pilot overview. In *Proceedings of the MultiLing 2013 Workshop on Multilingual Multi-document Summarization*, pages 29–38.

C. Y. Lin. 2004. Rouge: A package for automatic evaluation of summaries. *Proceedings of the Workshop on Text Summarization Branches Out (WAS 2004)*, pages 25–26.

Edward Loper and Steven Bird. 2002. Nltk: the natural language toolkit. *arXiv preprint cs/0205028.*

Annie Louis and Ani Nenkova. 2012. Automatically assessing machine summary content without a gold standard. *Computational Linguistics*, 39(2):267–300, Aug.

Nitin Madnani, Rebecca Passonneau, Necip Fazil Ayan, John M Conroy, Bonnie J Dorr, Judith L Klavans, Dianne P O'Leary, and Judith D Schlesinger. 2007. Measuring variability in sentence ordering for news summarization. In *Proceedings of the Eleventh European Workshop on Natural Language Generation*, pages 81–88. Association for Computational Linguistics.

Christopher Manning, Mihai Surdeanu, John Bauer, Jenny Finkel, Steven Bethard, and David McClosky. 2014. The stanford corenlp natural language processing toolkit. In *Proceedings of 52nd annual meeting of the association for computational linguistics: system demonstrations*, pages 55–60.

Nikiforos Pittaras, Stefano Montanelli, George Giannakopoulos, Alfio Ferrara, and Vangelis Karkaletsis. 2019. Crowdsourcing in single-document summary evaluation: The argo way. *Multilingual Text Analysis: Challenges, Models, And Approaches*, page 245.

Peter A. Rankel, John M. Conroy, Hoa Trang Dang, and Ani Nenkova. 2013. A decade of automatic content evaluation of news summaries: Reassessing the state of the art. In *Proceedings of the 51st Annual Meeting of the Association for Computational Linguistics (Volume 2: Short Papers)*, pages 131–136, Sofia, Bulgaria, August. Association for Computational Linguistics.

H. Saggion, J. M. Torres-Moreno, I. Cunha, and E. SanJuan. 2010. Multilingual summarization evaluation without human models. In *Proceedings of the 23rd International Conference on Computational Linguistics: Posters*, page 1059–1067.

Multi-lingual Wikipedia Summarization and Title Generation On Low Resource Corpus

Wei Liu, Lei Li, Zuying Huang and **Yinan Liu**
Center of Intelligence Science and Technology
School of Computer Science
Beijing University of Posts and Telecommunications
{thinkwee, leili, zoehuang, lyinan}@bupt.edu.cn

Abstract

MultiLing 2019 Headline Generation Task on Wikipedia Corpus raised a critical and practical problem: multilingual task on low resource corpus. In this paper we proposed Quality-Diversity Automatic Summarization(QDAS) model enhanced by sentence2vec and try to apply transfer learning based on large multilingual pre-trained language model for Wikipedia Headline Generation task. We treat it as sequence labeling task and develop two schemes to handle with it. Experimental results have shown that large pre-trained model can effectively utilize learned knowledge to extract certain phrase using low resource supervised data.

1 Introduction

MultiLing 2019 is an accepted RANLP 2019 workshop, focused on the multi-lingual aspect of summarization, but also its value across different settings. It holds three community tasks including: Headline Generation, Financial Narrative Summarization and Summary Evaluation. We have participated in the Wikipedia part of Headline Generation task, which is described as follows: Given Wikipedia articles from 42 language, for each article the title(Wikipedia Entry) and subtitles are masked with title length, as well as the summary. Researchers should reconstruct the title and subtitles of masked articles.

The classic seq2seq architecture for generating headlines is not suitable for this task since the given corpus is not large enough to train a seq2seq model from scratch for each language. Another downside of seq2seq is that it can not handle summarization tasks with large compression ratio, such as taking a whole Wikipedia arti-

cle as input and a title(usually a phrase) as output. So in this paper we propose a two-steps model for Wikipedia Headline Generation:

- **Reconstruct Summary: Extractive Summarization** Extract some sentences from the whole Wikipedia article to formulate summaries. We reconstruct titles based on the extracted summaries not the whole article.

- **Reconstruct Title: Sequence Labelling** Unlike other corpus, Wikipedia titles are phrases and can often be found in original sentences. So we transform this language generation task into sequence labeling task. For each summary sentence we try to mark some positions as title phrase and choose the best one.

2 Background

2.1 Summarization

Classification for automatic summarization is based on whether a sentence is from the raw document or not. Recently, brand-new proposed researches pay a lot attention to the abstractive summarization: applying structure and semantic methods to generate new sentences(Alfonseca et al., 2003) as summary is common in the early years, while it is now time for the neural network to perform. Seq2seq model(Lopyrev, 2015), as a typical abstractive summarization approach can map one long sentence (article) to another short sentence (summarization). However, an abstractive method is always limited in short papers and requires more advanced technology for natural language processing. As for long papers, for instance, single-document from Wikipedia, an extractive way seems like an easier and more convenient target, and this simple but robust method even gives its best shot when put into practical use.

Proceedings of the Multiling 2019 Workshop, co-located with the RANLP 2019 conference, pages 17–25
Varna, Bulgaria, September 6, 2019.
http://doi.org/10.26615/978-954-452-058-8_004

Thus, in this paper, we would like to adopt extractive summarization due to its increased feasibility.

2.2 Headline Generation

As a special application scenario of abstractive summarization, headline generation gains a lot of attention in recent years. In the HEADS(Colmenares et al., 2015) system researchers formulate the headline generation as a discrete optimization task in a feature-rich space. (Sun et al., 2015) combined extractive and abstractive summarization to detect a key event chain in article and generate titles based on it. (Takase et al., 2016) tried to incorporate structural syntactic and semantic information into a baseline neural attention-based model. There are also works focusing on extending sentence compression to document headline generation (Tan et al., 2017). Most of these works use seq2seq model, which is not suitable for Wikipedia Headline Generation task in MultiLing 2019 due to low resource multilingual training corpus. So we apply Pre-trained model to utilize the semantic knowledge learned in large unsupervised corpus on low-resource supervised task.

2.3 Pre-trained Language Model

Pre-trained Language Model(LM) is one of the most important research advances in Natural Language Processing(NLP) which focus on how to make use of language information in large corpus with unsupervised learning. Word2vec(Mikolov et al., 2013) and Glove(Pennington et al., 2014) have successfully learned semantic information in word embeddings and have been widely used in NLP tasks as inputs for model. Pre-trained language models explore more by learning syntactic and more abstractive features. These language models enrich embeddings information by adding encoders in pre-trained parts, producing context-aware representations when transfer to downstream tasks. Representative works including ULMFiT(Howard and Ruder, 2018), which captures general features of the language in different encoder layers to help text classification; ELMo(Peters et al., 2018), which learns embeddings from Bidirectional LSTM language models; BERT(Devlin et al., 2018), a successful application of training Transformer encoders on large masked corpus and reach eleven state-of-the-art results. After the release of BERT, many super-large-scale Transformer-Based models have

been raised including GPT-2(Radford et al., 2019), MASS(Song et al., 2019) and XLNet(Yang et al., 2019).

3 Pipeline Overview

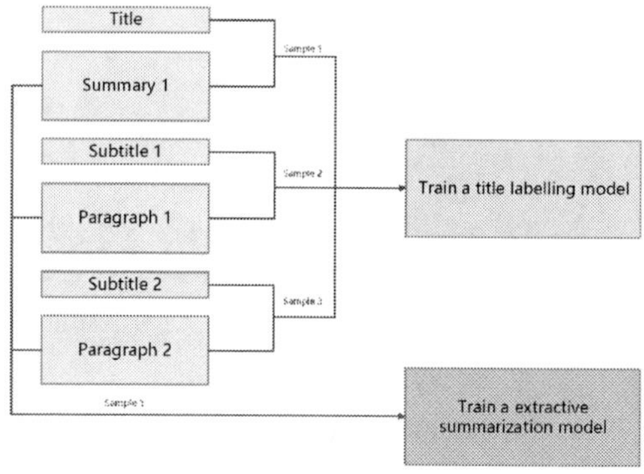

Figure 1: Pipeline overview during training. Red lines refer to samples for training a extractive summarization model and blue for training a title labelling model.

Figure 1 shows the pipeline during training. Given a Wikipedia article, The extractive summarization should extract summaries from paragraphs. The summarization model is unsupervised so actually there is no explicit training sample for summarization but we design features based on some statistics from paragraphs-summary pairs. For headline generation, we aim to provide sequence labelling data for model. In each article the title-summary and all subtitle-paragraph pairs are extracted to formulate training pairs. The process of transforming text pair into tagging sequence is described in section 7.

During test phrase, First we use summarization model to extract summaries from paragraphs and then for each sentence in the extracted summaries, title positions will be tagged out using the title labelling model. For subtitles, no summary is need and they are directly tagged out from corresponding paragraph sentences. There are maybe multiple candidate for each title or subtitle. The test corpus provides gold length so we pick up the candidate which has length closest to gold as final result.

4 Determinantal point processes

4.1 Definition

A discrete, finite point process P on a ground set D is a probability measure over its subsets, where determinant offers a kind of quantitatively analysis on this probability. P is called a determinantal point processDPPs if, when Y is a random subset drawn according to P, so that for every $A \subseteq D$:

$$P(A \subseteq \mathbf{Y}) = \det(K_A) \tag{1}$$

where $\mathbf{Y}$ is a specific instantation for random variable Y. That is to say, $\mathbf{Y}$ contains all the sentences the DPPs sampling method selects from the raw document. Set A provides a metric to measure the probability that two or more correlated sentences are extracted at the same time. The probability restriction is somehow related to a real symmetric matrix K that indexed by the elements of D.

Suppose there are N sentences in total, $D = \{x_1, x_2, ..., x_N\}$, here $K_A \equiv [k_{ij}]_{x_i, x_j \in A}$. Take $A = \{x_i, x_j\}$, then:

$$P(x_i, x_j \in \mathbf{Y}) = \begin{vmatrix} k_{ii} & k_{ij} \\ k_{ji} & k_{jj} \end{vmatrix} \tag{2}$$
$$= k_{ii}k_{jj} - k_{ij}k_{ji} \tag{3}$$

where k_{ij} or k_{ji} can be thought of the of similarity between sentences x_i and x_j, so that highly similar sentences are unlikely to appear together.

Since P is a probability measure, there are some frigid rules to obey when matrix K is constructed, i.e. K itself must be positive semidefinite to guarantee that all principal minors $\det(K_A)$ of K must be nonnegative; or $0 \leqslant K \leqslant I$, which ensures the probability to be in $[0, 1]$.

L-ensemble defines a DPP through another real, symmetric kernel L, also indexed by the elements of D:

$$P_L(\mathbf{Y} - Y) \propto \det(L_Y) \tag{4}$$

$$P_L(\mathbf{Y} = Y) = \frac{\det(L_Y)}{\det(L + I)} \tag{5}$$

To be clear, an L-ensemble is still a DPP, and its marginal kernel K is:

$$K = L(L + I)^{-1} = I - (L + I)^{-1} \tag{6}$$

L-ensemble provides an original method of scale to liberate the strict restriction on determinant, and (5) directly specifies the atomic probabilities for every possible instantiation of Y while K merely gives marginal probability of one certain item to be selected in one particular sampling process.

4.2 Quality vs. Diversity

Interpretability remains a common concern when we put a DPP into practical use. The DPP kernel L can be written as a Gram matrix:

$$L = B^{\top} B \tag{7}$$

where the columns of B are vectors representing sentences in the set D We now take this fact one step further, write each column B_i as the product of its norm q_i and a vector of normalized ϕ_i, so that the entries of the kernel can now be written as:

$$L_{ij} = q_i \phi_i^{\top} \phi_j q_j \tag{8}$$

We call q_i as a measure of quality of a sentence x_i, since the norm has a distance interpretation in Euclidean space. $\phi_i^{\top} \phi_j$ refers to a measure of similarity we assume S between sentences x_i and x_j.

In this way, we first calculate quality and similarity separately and then fuse them in a unified model to construct a kernel L. The determinant of a matrix, which the latter sampling process relies on, also has an intuitive geometric interpretation:

$$P_L(\mathbf{Y} - Y) \propto \det(L_Y) - Vol^2(\{B_i\}_{i \in Y}) \tag{9}$$

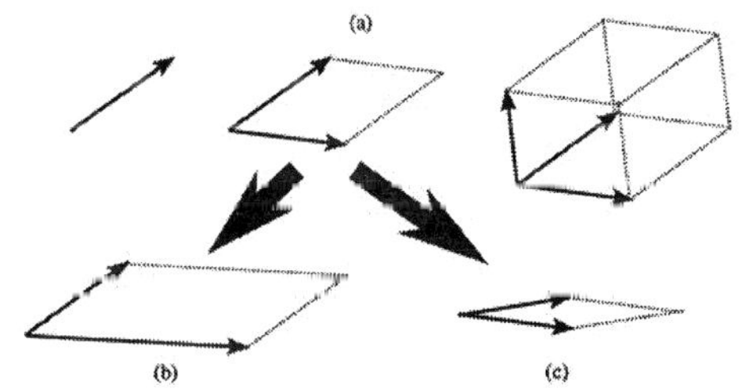

Figure 2: A geometric view of DPPs

Fig. 2.: Geometric view of DPPs (suppose there are two sentences in Y):
(a) The probability of a subset Y is the square of

the volume spanned by B_i and B_j.

(b) As quality increases, the norm stretches, so does the probability of subset containing sentence x_i.

(c) As two sentences x_i and x_j become more similar, the angle decreases, so does the probability containing both of them.

4.3 Sampling Algorithm

Input: q_i, S, D, max_len.

$quality\_vec = [q_i \text{ for } i \text{ in } D]$

matrix_L$= quality_vec * S * quality_vec^T$

$(\mathbf{v}_n, \lambda_n) =$ eigen_decompose(matrix_L)

$J = \emptyset$

for $n = 1, 2, \ldots, N$ **do**

$\quad J = J \cup \{n\}$ with prob. $\frac{\lambda_n}{\lambda_n + 1}$

$\quad V = \{\mathbf{v}_n\}_{n \in J}$

End for

$Y = \emptyset$

While $|V| > 0$ **do**

$\quad$ Select i^{th} sentence from D

$\qquad$ with $Pr(i) = \frac{1}{|V|} \sum_{v \in V} (\mathbf{v}^\top \mathbf{e}_i)^2$

$\quad Y = Y \cup D[i]$

$\quad V = V_\perp$, an orthonormal basis for the

$\qquad\qquad$ subspace of V orthogonal to e_i

$\quad |V| --$

End While

Output: summary Y

An expected sample result based on the determinant of kernel L takes not only quality of items but also the interior cohesion into account. In order to explain the sampling algorithm more precisely, there are some extra principle properties of DPPs worth to be mentioned.

- A DPP with kernel L is a mixture of elementary DPPs

- If Y is drawn according to an elementary DPP with a set of orthonormal vectors $\mathbf{v}_i, i = 1, 2, ..., k, k < N$, then $|Y| = |V|$. Also, let $\lambda_i, i = 1, 2, ..., N$ be the eigenvalues of L, then $|Y|$ is distributed as the number of successes in N Bernoulli trials where trial n succeeds with probability $\frac{\lambda_n}{\lambda_n + 1}$.

A DPP is called elementary if every eigenvalue of its marginal kernel is either 0 or 1, so that all principal minors $\det(K_A)$ is either 0 or 1, due to the fact that determinant equals the product of all eigenvalues. The multiplication of any normalized

vector and its transpose $\mathbf{v}\mathbf{v}^\top$ happens to be a matrix with such property. Since we have already obtained the kernel L and its corresponding eigenvectors, based on the conversion relationship between kernel L and marginal kernel K according to (6), this theory points out another representation of marginal probability of A in a mixture way.

$$P(A \subseteq \mathbf{Y}) = \det(K_A) = \det\left(\sum_1^N \frac{\lambda_n}{\lambda_n + 1} W_n\right) \quad (10)$$

where W_i was spanned by the eigenvector from kernel L of corresponding sentence x_i in A, and λ_i refers to its eigenvalue.

From these two properties above, we notice that a DPP is initially defined through marginal kernel with continuous probability in $[0, 1]$, while a elementary one provides merely two outcomes: to be selected or not. This perhaps inspires the sampling process to choose an elementary DPP with probability equal to its mixture component in the first loop, and the cardinality $|Y|(= |V|)$ is determined meanwhile. To be clear, the mixture way can be regarded as the mathematical expectation from multiple trials, but when it comes to an instantiation, selection with probability is used to simulate the results from Bernoulli distribution.

A sample Y is produced during the second loop phase. Since the new elementary theory is also defined through determinants, using its analogical geometric interpretation by the base * height formula for the volume of a parallelepiped we have:

$$Vol^2(\{B_i\}_{i \in Y}) = \|B_1\| Vol(\{Proj_\perp e_1\}_{i=2}^k) \quad (11)$$

where B_1 denotes the 1st sentence to be selected, e_1 stands for its one-hot representation and $Proj_\perp e_1$ refers to the projection operator onto the subspace orthogonal to e_1. Assume we have already selected the best B_1, and then the V need to be updated to an orthonormal basis for the subspace of the original V perpendicular to e_1 for diversity. Proceeding inductively, the loop goes on. During each iteration, the first vector in V that contributes to the norm of B_1, which makes its quality the best, is eliminated.

5 Reconstruct Summary

Our Quality-Diversity Automatic Summarization (QDAS) framework merely requires general preprocessing like sentence splitting and word segmentation, and then it can be applied in multilingual environment. When it comes to document representation, first we construct matrix L from holistic perspectives, through $L_{ij} = B_i^\top B_j$ from Sent2Vec directly. Furthermore, we build matrix L from partial perspectives, through $L_{ij} = q_i S_{ij} q_j$ concretely. we extract quality q_i for a sentence, and calculate cosine similarity S_{ij} between every two sentences. Given the matrix L, the sampling method based on DPPs introduced by Kulesza and Taskar (Kulesza et al., 2012) ($O(N^2)$) can automatically choose diverse sentences with high quality. When constructing a semantic space using embedding expressions, quality refers to the length of a vector in the semantic space. Sentences that indicate strong semantic feature are called high quality and preferred for summarization.

6 Reconstruct Title

We use two kinds of BERT(Devlin et al., 2018)(Bidirectional Encoder Representations from Transformers) Based sequence labeling schemes to label the title phrases, which are CRF Model and NMT Model. We developed our code based on sberbank-ai's open source project[1].

6.1 Baseline

Based on the fact that most titles in Wikipedia articles are entries or concepts that often appear in the first sentence, we set up two simple but effective baselines to extract titles:

- **NER** Use Named Entity Recognition to extract named entities in the first sentence of summary. We simply choose the first entity as title.

- **SUB** Based on dependency parse we found the subject of the first sentence in summary and choose it as title.

We use Spacy(Honnibal and Montani, 2017) to perform the NER extraction and dependency parsing.

6.2 BERT

BERT is used to formulate the encoder of sequence labeling model. It is trained for language modeling task on large corpus and can be easily applied to several natural language tasks, using its token embeddings or sentence embeddings.

BERT consists of multiple bidirectional Transformer layers and perform two unsupervised tasks on large corpus:

- Masked LM: standard conditional language models can not been trained in two directions since tokens would indirectly "see itself" in multi-layer bidirectional model. BERT randomly mask some tokens and predict these masked tokens. Furthermore, to prevent the mismatch problem between pre-training and fine-tuning, BERT do not simply mask the token to the symbol $[MASK]$, but replace the chosen token with (1) the $[MASK]$ 80% of the time (2) a random token 10% of the time (3) the unchanged token 10% of the time.

- Next Sentence Prediction: to capture the syntactic and context-aware information of language, BERT adds a sentence-level task: a binarized next sentence prediction task. Adjacent sentence pairs are fed to BERT and only 50% of the time the second sentence is the actual next sentence that follows the first sentence. 50% of the time it is a random sentence from the corpus.

The input representation is sentence pairs that are packed together into a single sequence. The first token of every sequence is a special classification token($[CLS]$) which has final hidden state as the aggregate sequence representation for classification task. Sentence pairs are separated by a special token($[SEP]$). The input embedding for each token contains three parts: Token Embedding, Segment Embedding and Position Embedding.

We chose official pre-trained Multilingual Cased Base version of BERT as encoder for sentences, which has 110M parameters developed on 104 languages. We make sequence labeling data using sentences from gold summaries. The multilingual BERT model can use data from all 42 languages instead of training separate model for each language. The pre-trained BERT can be fixed as a "context-aware embedding look-up table" or fine-tuned together with downstream model. We chose the former way for two reasons:

- The task dataset are the same as pre-trained BERT data source, which is Wikipedia.

- The supervised training set is too small for the whole BERT model to transfer. Fine-tuning will make sharp parameters adjustments which harms the performance of pre-trained model.

---

[1] https://github.com/sberbank-ai/ner-bert

6.3 BERT Based CRF Model

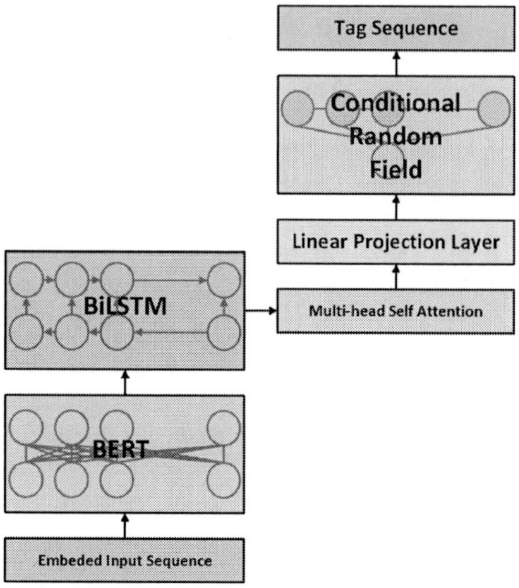

Figure 3: Bert Based CRF Model

The representations for all tokens in a sequence from BERT's last layer are fed to decoder for tagging title phrase. The encoded information are first fed to a bidirectional LSTM layer then a multi-head self attention layer and a liner projection layer to generate tag probabilities. Last a CRF(Conditional Random Field)(Lafferty et al., 2001) layer is added to adjust the tag sequence. The model architecture is shown in Figure 3.

6.4 BERT Based NMT Model

The BERT Based NMT(Neural Machine Translation) Model is almost the same as BERT Based CRF Model except for the decoder. NMT model uses sequence to sequence architecture to generate tag sequence. The encoded information from BERT and bidirectional LSTM is decoded by a unidirectional LSTM decoder. Classic attention mechanism using dot alignment function is applied between encoder and decoder to focus on different parts of encoded information when generate one tag. The decoder also accept decoder input embeddings, which is the same as encoder input embeddings. The model architecture is shown in Figure 4.

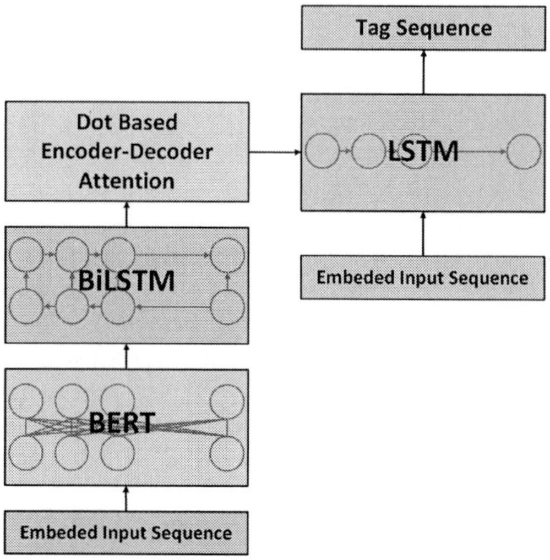

Figure 4: Bert Based NMT Model

7 Experimental Setup

The MultiLing 2019 Headline Generation task provides 9293 Wikipedia articles from 42 languages. Most of the languages have only 30 articles for training. Several languages have more articles. The details are shown in table 1.

Language	# Articles
EN	3793
DE	2112
ES	1024
HE	639
IT	277
ZH	178
AR	175
JA	51

Table 1: Dataset overview(only show parts of 42 languages which have more than 30 articles) .

Usually the title of a Wikipedia article is a entry which is defined in the first sentence of summary. So we check every sentence in gold summary and pick up those sentences with title included. Then like other sequence labeling tasks we use BIO symbols to tag the position where title appears. We use symbol $[B\_MISC]$ to mark the beginning of the title phrase and $[I\_MISC]$ to mark rest parts of the title. We collect 26494 samples and make a language-wise division to generate train/valid/test dataset by a ratio of 8:1:1.

Subtitles(headers) in articles are more flexible than entries and can not be extracted directly. Those languages with large training corpus like English may train a seq2seq model but most low resource languages can not train a independent model. So we just use the same sequence labeling model to tag subtitles. When test each subtitle will try to tag on sentences from the corresponding paragraph.

Model	BERT+CRF	BERT+NMT
L(BERT)	12	12
H(BERT)	768	768
A(BERT)	12	12
A(Encoder)	3	-
H(BiLSTM)	256	256
H(LSTM)	-	256
E	-	128
# Parameters	1150675	1908755

Table 2: Hyperparameter setup for BERT based models.

We denote the number of BERT Transformer layers as L, the hidden size as H, the number of self-attention heads as A, the embedding hidden size as E. The hyperparameter setup is shown in table 2. The Hyperparameters stay the same as Google's version of BERT. We use the default setting of sberbank-ai on designing the BiLSTM and LSTM. Both BERT models are trained for 10 epochs, from which we observed that the validation precision can not be improved more.

8 Results

8.1 Extractive Summarization

We generate a single document summary first for all the given Wikipedia feature articles on training set from 42 languages provided. We use ROUGE package that measures skip n-gram overlap with the golden summaries for evaluation; we provide F-measure results and denote them by ROUGE1, ROUGE2 and ROUGE-F. The results are listed below in table 3.

From the table 3 we can see that even on corpus with low corpus the extracted summaries still get high ROUGE scores due to the unsupervised method. The top four results in the table have been bolded and the score reached nearly 0.5.

Language	ROUGE1	ROUGE2	ROUGE-L
AF	0.36309	0.07003	0.17838
AR	0.32613	0.05661	0.12668
AZ	0.17838	0.17838	0.08077
BG	0.31729	0.05438	0.14489
BS	0.20603	0.02805	0.10914
CA	0.41166	0.10017	0.16878
CS	0.36954	0.06100	0.13375
DE	0.34239	0.05847	0.16809
EL	0.42561	0.10546	0.22027
EN	0.46123	0.12328	0.19016
EO	0.32418	0.06765	0.17613
ES	**0.50390**	**0.14792**	**0.24045**
EU	0.18970	0.03056	0.09727
FA	0.37201	0.07671	0.15731
FI	0.18228	0.02617	0.09727
FR	**0.48166**	**0.15034**	**0.24975**
HE	0.18020	0.03957	0.09027
HR	0.23411	0.02854	0.11514
ID	0.32536	0.06755	0.13595
IT	0.40780	0.09950	0.20031
JA	0.38426	0.09298	0.17918
JV	0.24805	0.03990	0.12624
KA	0.17031	0.03514	0.09736
KO	0.22891	0.03904	0.10062
LI	0.22833	0.02795	0.12987
LV	0.19157	0.02774	0.09728
MR	**0.50092**	**0.15771**	**0.23461**
MS	0.29083	0.06304	0.13938
NL	0.37004	0.07344	0.17570
NN	0.27399	0.02045	0.13399
NO	0.35866	0.04805	0.14446
PL	0.31028	0.05631	0.14301
PT	**0.49376**	**0.16303**	**0.24452**
RO	0.38691	0.07458	0.15742
RU	0.26514	0.04773	0.12516
SK	0.21378	0.02534	0.09533
TH	0.46316	0.16334	0.16393
TR	0.26181	0.05757	0.10476
TT	0.12043	0.01173	0.06345
UK	0.12143	0.01198	0.06975
VI	0.45210	0.14085	0.15224
ZH	0.31551	0.06381	0.12747

Table 3: Performance on MultiLing Single-document Summarization

8.2 Entry Extraction

All results shown in this section are precision of predicting the title, not including subtitles.

First we test our unsupervised rule-based baselines. The Spacy toolkit can only support parts of the languages so we just collect results on these languages. Table 4 shows that on certain languages like DE, FR and PT, the first entity in the first sentence of summary can point out the entry of whole Wikipedia article with a probability of about 0.4. Even though the entry is not the first entity, we identify the subject entity using dependency parsing and get better results. The results from baselines prove that about half of the samples make a explicit description for the entry in the first sentence.

precision	NER	SUB
EN	0.105	0.507
DE	0.48	0.49
ES	0.013	0.451
FR	0.397	0.4
IT	0.021	0.523
PT	0.404	0.433
EL	-	0.4
NL	-	0.567
RU	0.25	-

Table 4: Results of Baselines. '-' means that Spacy does not support this language on NER or dependency parsing tasks.

	precision	recall	f1-score
B_MISC	0.779	0.603	0.680
I_MISC	0.721	0.668	0.693
micro avg	0.753	0.629	0.686
macro avg	0.750	0.635	0.687
weighted avg	0.755	0.629	0.685

Table 5: Results of BERT Based CRF Model.

As for BERT Based models, BIO precision shows that compared to baselines, BERT Based CRF model learned more rules to label the entry of an article and gains great precision improvement. The model is trained and tested on a language-mixed and shuffled dataset. We randomly divide the dataset for ten times and calculate the average precision.

The CRF Model reaches 0.779 and 0.721 precision on $[B\_MISC]$ and $[I\_MISC]$, which is a average precision on all 42 languages. It proves that CRF Model can make full use of pre-trained language model and perform well on low resource languages. The span precision, recall and f1-score of CRF Model are 0.703, 0.607 and 0.651 respectively.

The NMT Model reaches 0.810 and 0.782 precision on MISC tags. The span precision, recall and f1-score of CRF Model are 0.755, 0.780 and 0.767 respectively. The NMT Model outperforms CRF Model on all metrics.

Both the CRF and NMT Model reaches f1-score higher than baselines. It is worth noting that the f1-score is an average on all 42 languages and the baseline can only perform on few languages, which proves that the BERT based model can learn common syntactic rules from multilingual corpus and transfer well on low resource languages.

	precision	recall	f1-score
B_MISC	0.810	0.802	0.806
I_MISC	0.782	0.840	0.810
micro avg	0.798	0.817	0.808
macro avg	0.796	0.821	0.808
weighted avg	0.799	0.817	0.808

Table 6: Results of BERT Based NMT Model.

Although BERT are not pre-trained for language generation task like Neural Machine Translation, the BERT Based NMT Model still gets higher precision compared to CRF Model. There may be several reasons:

- Compared to CRF Model, NMT model incorporate another LSTM as decoder which expand the total amount of parameters and have large capacity when fitting data.

- NMT model uses embeded sequence as input both on encoder and decoder. With two supervised signal input the NMT can converge better than CRF Model when training the same epochs.

The NMT Model gets 4 points higher precision both on BIO precision and span precision compared to CRF Model.

9 Conclusion

We proposed a two-steps model for Wikipedia Headline Generation task. First we extract summaries that contain the key information of the whole article then a sequence labelling model using pre-trained language model is applied to further pick up key entry phrases. We test our extractive summarization model and sequence labelling model independently and reach good results compared to baselines.

References

Enrique Alfonseca, José María Guirao, and Antonio Moreno-Sandoval. 2003. Description of the uam system for generating very short summaries at duc-2003. In *DUC 2003: Document Understanding Conference, May 31–June 1, 2003, Edmonton, Canada.*

Carlos A Colmenares, Marina Litvak, Amin Mantrach, and Fabrizio Silvestri. 2015. Heads: Headline generation as sequence prediction using an abstract feature-rich space. In *Proceedings of the 2015 Conference of the North American Chapter of the Association for Computational Linguistics: Human Language Technologies*. pages 133–142.

Jacob Devlin, Ming-Wei Chang, Kenton Lee, and Kristina Toutanova. 2018. Bert: Pre-training of deep bidirectional transformers for language understanding. *arXiv preprint arXiv:1810.04805* .

Matthew Honnibal and Ines Montani. 2017. spacy 2: Natural language understanding with bloom embeddings, convolutional neural networks and incremental parsing. *To appear* 7.

Jeremy Howard and Sebastian Ruder. 2018. Universal language model fine-tuning for text classification. *arXiv preprint arXiv:1801.06146* .

Alex Kulesza, Ben Taskar, et al. 2012. Determinantal point processes for machine learning. *Foundations and Trends® in Machine Learning* 5(2–3):123–286.

John Lafferty, Andrew McCallum, and Fernando CN Pereira. 2001. Conditional random fields: Probabilistic models for segmenting and labeling sequence data .

Konstantin Lopyrev. 2015. Generating news headlines with recurrent neural networks. *arXiv preprint arXiv:1512.01712* .

Tomas Mikolov, Ilya Sutskever, Kai Chen, Greg S Corrado, and Jeff Dean. 2013. Distributed representations of words and phrases and their compositionality. In *Advances in neural information processing systems*. pages 3111–3119.

Jeffrey Pennington, Richard Socher, and Christopher Manning. 2014. Glove: Global vectors for word representation. In *Proceedings of the 2014 conference on empirical methods in natural language processing (EMNLP)*. pages 1532–1543.

Matthew E Peters, Mark Neumann, Mohit Iyyer, Matt Gardner, Christopher Clark, Kenton Lee, and Luke Zettlemoyer. 2018. Deep contextualized word representations. *arXiv preprint arXiv:1802.05365* .

Alec Radford, Jeffrey Wu, Rewon Child, David Luan, Dario Amodei, and Ilya Sutskever. 2019. Language models are unsupervised multitask learners. *OpenAI Blog* 1(8).

Kaitao Song, Xu Tan, Tao Qin, Jianfeng Lu, and Tie-Yan Liu. 2019. Mass: Masked sequence to sequence pre-training for language generation. *arXiv preprint arXiv:1905.02450* .

Rui Sun, Yue Zhang, Meishan Zhang, and Donghong Ji. 2015. Event-driven headline generation. In *Proceedings of the 53rd Annual Meeting of the Association for Computational Linguistics and the 7th International Joint Conference on Natural Language Processing (Volume 1: Long Papers)*. pages 462–472.

Sho Takase, Jun Suzuki, Naoaki Okazaki, Tsutomu Hirao, and Masaaki Nagata. 2016. Neural headline generation on abstract meaning representation. In *Proceedings of the 2016 conference on empirical methods in natural language processing*. pages 1054–1059.

Jiwei Tan, Xiaojun Wan, and Jianguo Xiao. 2017. From neural sentence summarization to headline generation: A coarse-to-fine approach. In *IJCAI*. pages 4109–4115.

Zhilin Yang, Zihang Dai, Yiming Yang, Jaime Carbonell, Ruslan Salakhutdinov, and Quoc V Le. 2019. Xlnet: Generalized autoregressive pretraining for language understanding. *arXiv preprint arXiv:1906.08237* .

A topic-based sentence representation for extractive text summarization

Nikolaos Gialitsis
DIT, NKUA
nikolasyal@gmail.com

Nikiforos Pittaras
DIT, NKUA
IIT, NCSR-D
npittaras@di.uoa.gr

Panagiotis Stamatopoulos
DIT, NKUA
takis@di.uoa.gr

Abstract

We examine the effect of probabilistic topic model-based word representations, on sentence-based extractive summarization. We formulate the task of sentence selection as a binary classification problem, and we test a variety of machine learning algorithms, exploring a range of different settings for classification and modelling. A preliminary investigation via a wide experimental evaluation on the MultiLing 2015 MSS dataset illustrates that topic-based representations can prove beneficial to the extractive summarization process, compared to a TF-IDF baseline, with Quadratic Discriminant Analysis and Gradient Boosting providing the best results for micro and macro F1 score, respectively.

1 Introduction

In recent years, advances in the field of Natural Language Processing (NLP) have revolutionized the way machines are used to interpret human-written text. With the rapid accumulation of publicly available documents, from newspaper articles to social media posts, machine learning methods designed to automate data analysis are urgently needed. A problem that has been relevant since the dawn of NLP is the automatic summary extraction from a large corpus of text. The development of a consistent and time-efficient method of extractive summarization can assist journalists in their day to day tasks, as well as provide better tools for information retrieval.

Summaries need to be as brief as possible but must also capture the important elements of a text. This turns out to be a challenging task for any algorithm to carry out, since there is a virtually infinite number of documents that can exist, and each one of them can refer to a unique concept. Natural language is tricky for a computer to model; the absence or presence of a single word can shift the meaning of a whole sentence or even of a whole chapter. On the other hand, some words do not add any value to a sentence, the meaning is still the same even if we ignore them. To make matters even more complex, a word can be crucial for one article but of little importance to another.

Human brains have evolved to effectively detect complex patterns in text, to focus on the most important bits of a text while ignoring those that are less important. For a machine, the importance of word or a sentence is not obvious, as it needs to be programmed with a built-in way to assess it in any given context. For the purposes of summary extraction, an automatic summarizer needs to be able to compare words, or sentences via computational means, and announce those with the highest scores as the most relevant for a given document. The representation, aka. the method by which these similarity scores are assigned, is of critical importance to any summary extraction task.

When the representation is selected, the next step is training the model, that is, feeding the sentences represented as numerical sequences, to a machine learning procedure. If the representation and the dataset are suitable for the goal we are trying to accomplish, we can expect that the model will be able to predict which words or sentences are more important to a given document. Summing up all the sentences that the model considers to be important, results in a summary of the input text.

2 Related work

2.1 Topic Modeling

Proceedings of the Multiling 2019 Workshop, co-located with the RANLP 2019 conference, pages 26–34
Varna, Bulgaria, September 6, 2019.
http://doi.org/10.26615/978-954-452-058-8_005

2.1.1 Semantic Topics.

Topics can be viewed as semantic groups that refer to a particular portion of reality. A document can refer to one or more distinct topics, which humans can often easily distinguish. For example, the words "fishing", "boat", "waves", have something in common; they are all affiliated with the sea. We can think of Sea as one topic, which contains these three words. However, topics are not always that identifiable and there can be broader or narrower topics. Resuming the previous example, alternatively, there can exist a topic on fishing , another one on boats and another one on ocean waves. Each one of them contains a number of words that are directly tied to that concept.

As demonstrated, there is no unique way to infer topics from an input document. It depends on the representation, the way that we measure the similarity scores between two words.It only makes sense that if two words are similar, they will have a high chance of belonging to the same topic.This statement derives from the distributional hypothesis in linguistics which proposes that words that occur in similar contexts tend to have similar meanings (Harris, 1954) However, we have to keep in mind that one word can also belong to one or more topics and that the number of topics in a document is also not known.

2.1.2 Latent Dirichlet Allocation.

Topic models can infer topics by observing the distribution of words across documents. This can be accomplished with Latent Dirichlet Allocation (LDA) (Steyvers and Griffiths, 2017; Blei, 2012), a generative statistical model that makes the hypothesis that there exists an underlying distribution of words,topics and documents, which generated the input text collection. Using probabilistic topic model jargon, the words of a document are called "observed variables", whereas the variables of the topic structure are called "hidden variables". Using an iterative process, the model estimates the posterior distribution of the hidden variables given the observed variables. However, the vast amount of topic structures that can exist result in exponential complexities of computation. For this reason, sampling-based algorithms have been developed , such as Gibbs sampling.

2.1.3 Gibbs sampling

In Gibbs sampling (Steyvers and Griffiths, 2017), a Markov chain (i.e., a sequence of random variables, each only dependent on the previous) is constructed, using samples from the distribution of hidden variables. The assignment of words to topics is sampled iteratively until the Markov chain converges to the target distribution. In the beginning of this procedure, each word is randomly assigned to a topic and in each subsequent iteration, the word-topic assignments are re-evaluated, which might result in words passing through multiple topics during the process.

2.2 Vector Space Models

Vector Space Model (VSM) approaches project the input to a n-dimensional vector representation, where the semantic similarity of the points is determined by their distance (e.g cosine, euclidean, etc.) in the projected vector space. Feature vector representations are widely used in Machine Learning tasks, e.g. for classification, clustering, etc. of a collection of input items (Turney and Pantel, 2010).

2.2.1 Bag-of-words approaches

A popular way to represent a set of documents as feature vectors has been the bag-of-words approach (Salton et al., 1975), where a sentence can be represented as a vector of word features. Each vector coordinate expresses word statistics, such as frequency or the Term Frequency-Inverse Document Frequency (TF-IDF) (Jones, 2004) value of a given word in the source texts. By mapping a word to its TF-IDF value, words receive a high weight when they appear often in the referenced document, but rarely in other documents of the set. The benefit of this approach is that it suppresses common words that appear in the majority of documents, without containing any semantic value for the task. It has been demonstrated that the approach can result in significant improvements over raw frequency approaches in a variety of information retrieval tasks. (Salton and Buckley, 1988).

2.3 Extractive Summarization

In extractive summarization, the summaries produced contain a subset of unmodified sentences contained in the original documents. Consequently, in these approaches, sentences, and not words, consist the units of feature selection. The pipeline of an extractive text summarizer is

formed of three relatively independent tasks :
(Rao and Gudivada, 2018)

1. Construction of an intermediate representation of the input text based on the key aspects of the text
2. Scoring the sentences based on the selected representation
3. Selection of the summary comprising of a number of sentences

Gupta and Lehal(2010) define a different division of tasks, which includes a pre-processing and a processing step. The pre-processing step also includes: sentence boundary identification, stop-word elimination, and stemming. During the processing step, weights are assigned to specific sentence features by a feature-wise weighting mechanism, with the top ranked sentences being included in the final summary. In this study, we will follow the paradigm, proposed by Rao and Gudivada(2018).

There are two types of representation-based approaches: 1) topic representations and indicator representations. A Topic representation transforms the text into an intermediate form and interprets the topic(s) discussed in the text. The techniques used for this, differ in terms of their complexity, and are divided into frequency-driven approaches, topic word approaches, latent semantic analysis and Bayesian topic models. Indicator representation describes every sentence as a list of formal features (indicators) of importance such as sentence length, position in the document, or having certain phrases; the use of indicators was demonstrated by J et al.(2008).

2.3.1 Sentence-based summarization

In contrast to bag-of-words representations that suffer from the curse of dimensionality (Bellman, 1958), more sophisticated recent approaches produce sentence vectors in a lower dimensional space , such as a latent-topic space. Many such these methods utilize topic clusters in order to locate the centroids (or medoids in non-euclidean spaces) that best represent the sentences in the topics. Then the score of each sentence is assigned in respect to its distance from the clusters' representatives. For example, Thomas et al.(2015) used a graph-based procedure where each node of the graph represents a sentence and the edges' weights reflect the similarity between the connected nodes. Next, a PageRank/TextRank algorithm is applied

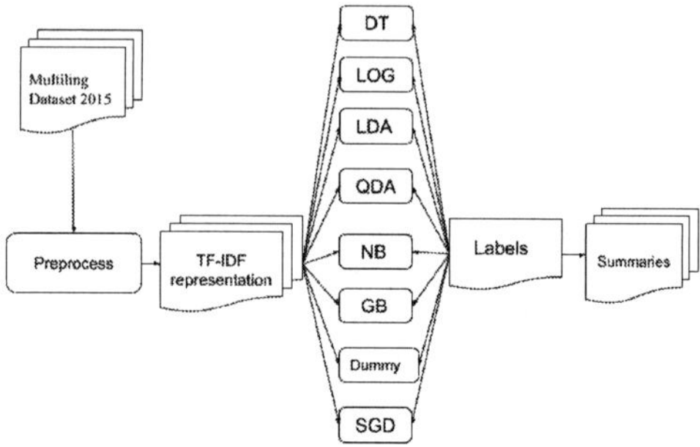

Figure 1: The pipeline for the TF-IDF-based extractive summarization

to extract the sentence representatives based on the graph centrality. In another topic-based approach,featured by Vicente et al. (2015) Principal Component Analysis (PCA) was used to project the sentences into a lower-dimension space. The principal components are then evaluated and the sentences with the highest scores get selected to appear in the summary.

2.3.2 Contributions

There are some limitations with the majority of the existing topic-based summarization methods. First, they work directly in the sentence space and the term-topic information embedded in the sentences is ignored.

In this study, we combine the simplicity of word-level approaches with the power of probabilistic topic models; instead of limiting word information to a single value (e.g. frequency or TF-IDF weight), we model sentences with word-level topic assignments. This approach is supported by a clear and rigorous probabilistic interpretation (rather than some ad-hoc sentence-level aggregation of a multitude of unrelated scores) and produces rich, semantic sentence-level representations.

3   Proposed Method

3.1   Binary classification modelling

Extractive summarization can be modelled as a binary classification problem, where one class represents the sentences to be included in the summary, and the other one the sentences that should be ignored. More formally, a document comprised of N sentences $S = \{s_i\}, i \in \{1, \ldots N\}$ is

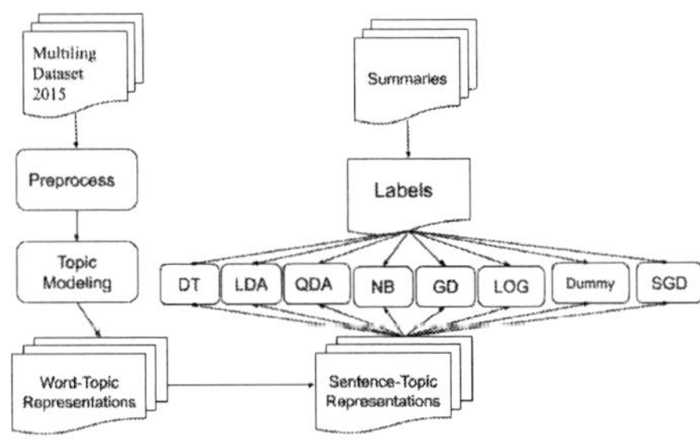

Figure 2: pipeline for topic-modeling based extractive summarization

transformed to a subset of M sentence summaries $O = \{o_j\}, o_j \in S, j \in \{1 \dots M\}$ via a classifier that maps each sentence to a binary label (denoted inclusion in the summary or not). The classification model should select O such that the concatenation of its sentences should produce a coherent, non-reductive and readable summary.

In this study, we tackle classification as a supervised learning procedure; it is necessary to have a set of ground truth sentences, that is, sentences that are indeed valid summaries of input documents. Such data (commonly referred to as "golden" summaries) are manually compiled by humans, who are considered the best summarizers (Genest et al., 2009); if a human reader can not differentiate between a human summarizer and an automatic summarizer, that means that the extractive model is optimal. Using the input documents and ground truth data, the classification system can facilitate learning using input sentence features towards a saliency detection model that implements sentence selection towards extractive summarization. We detail this process in the next sections.

3.2 Topic-based Sentence Extraction

In our approach of extractive summarization, we utilize the topics' information in word-level feature vector representations using an LDA-based topic model with Gibbs sampling.

The intuition behind our proposed method follows two statements:(1) the significance of a word is reflected by its contribution to a set of semantic topics (2) the significance of a sentence is reflected by patterns in its words-topics contributions.

For the purpose of formality we provide the mathematical description of the proposed method.

Given a finite set of semantic topics $T = \{T_1, T_2, ...T_{|T|}\}$ over the documents' space D, a set of sentences per document $S_{D_i} = \{s_1, s_2, ..., s_k\}$, and a set of words per sentence $W_{S_{D_i}} = \{w_1, w_2, ...w_n\}$, we define the word-topics contribution function of a word w as:

$$C(w) = \left[p(w, T_1), p(w, T_2), ...p(w, T_{|T|}) \right] \quad (1)$$

where the vector $C(w)$ is the contribution of the word w to the topics set T and $p(w, T_i)$ is the probability of w being generated by the topic $T_i \in T$ (after the topic model has inferred the posterior probability distributions), as defined by LDA's term-topic distribution. In simpler terms, this probability is computed using:

$$p(w, T_i) = \frac{N(w, T_i)}{N(T_i)} \quad (2)$$

where $N(w, T_i)$ and $N(T_i)$ are the number of occurences of w in T_i and the total number of word occurences in T_i, respectively.

Further, normalization is applied over the contributions of each word vector, in order to project the values into the $\{0, 1\}$ interval, dividing each value by the maximum value in each vector :

$$C_i(w) = \frac{C_i(w)}{max(C(w))} \forall i \in \{1, |T|\} \quad (3)$$

where $max(C(w)) \neq 0$

After all word-topic contributions have been calculated, each sentence $s = \{w_1, w_2, ..., w_n\}$ is represented by the vector

$$C(s) = [C(w_1), C(w_2), ..., C(w_n)], \quad (4)$$

effectively transforming an input set of sentences $S = \{s_1, s_2, ..s_k\}$ into the multi-dimensional vector

$$S' = [C(s_1), C(s_2), ..., C(s_k)] \quad (5)$$

Since most machine learning algorithms work with data of equal dimensionality, we apply padding to enforce a uniform dimension accross sentences. In zero-padding, the smaller-sized vectors are appended with zeros until all vectors have the same number of dimensions. Since there can be sentences with different dimensions in the documents examined, we implement zero-padding, in order for the elements of S' in equation (5) to become uniform.

4 Experiments

4.1 Dataset and Preprocessing

We use the Multiling 2015 dataset for single-document summarization (Giannakopoulos et al., 2015) [1]. The dataset is constructed by the MultiLing community (Conroy et al., 2015) from wikipedia pages, using articles annotated by human-curated summaries. It consists of 40 languages, spanning 30 documents and summary sets – in our work, we restrict the evaluation to the English language, i.e. work with the 30 English documents provided.

We modify the dataset in order to align it with the extractive summarization setting (as the provided summaries are not purely document sentences). First, the ground truth is modified, labelling input source sentences with a label $l \in 0, 1$ (1 if the sentence should be included in the summary, else 0). This is computed by measuring the similarity of each source sentence with each human-authored summary for the document, in terms of common n-grams. I.e, each human-authored sentence g_i is assigned to a maximally similar source sentence s_j. Stopword filtering is applied prior to this process, and each source sentence is assigned to at most one ground truth sentence.

Additionally, since the dataset used contains very unbalanced classes – the grand majority (with a ratio approximately 13 to 1) belonging to class 0, i.e. the class for sentences that should not be included in the summaries. To alleviate this, we employ an oversampling scheme. To limit the bias towards class 0 during the training phase of our model, we implemented oversampling, by repeating the sentences belonging to class 1 a fixed number of times arriving at a 2 : 1 negative to positive ratio, at most. This way, a classifier that always predicts dominant label (in this case 0) has suboptimal performance.

Also, all letters were converted to lower-case in order for the model not to differentiate between words in the beginning and in the middle of sentences, such as "apples" and "Apples". In addition, stop words were also removed from the vocabulary to limit its size, without significant loss

	train	test
mean num. sentences	233	184.9
mean summ. sentences	77.9	13.5
mean num. words	25.5	22.8
sample sentences	6990	5546

Table 1: Multiling 2015 single-document summarization dataset characteristics.

of information.

Other preprocessing tasks such as stemming was also explored; however, they did not have a significant effect on the classification performance. After these steps, we end up with the final version of the dataset which is described in detail in table 1.

4.2 Evaluation

We use the provided training and test dataset portion to train and evaluate the produced classifiers. The evaluation is performed in terms of micro and macro F-measure; the former is calculated by counting the total true positives, false negatives and false positives while the macro-averaged variant calculates metrics for each label, and finds their unweighted mean (i.e., not considering label imbalance). Additionally, we compare the predicted summaries with the ground-truth as described in section 4.1, using the Rouge metric to assess performance (Lin, 2004) [2]. Rouge scores reflect the overlap of n-grams between the ground-truth and the predicted summaries.

4.3 TF-IDF Sentence Classification

As a baseline model, we also implemented a TF-IDF representation of the input dataset. The TF-IDF scores for each word-document pair are calculated and each sentence is represented by the vector of the tf-idf values of the words it contains. For example, a sentence with N words results in a N_w-dimensional vector, where N_w is the number of words in the sentence.

The pipeline for sentences classification using the tf-idf approach is summarized schematically in Figure 1.The scikit-learn v0.21.3 machine learning library [3] is used for building and training the models.

---

[1] http://multiling.iit.demokritos.gr/ pages/view/1516/multiling-2015

[2] https://pypi.org/project/py-rouge/
[3] https://scikit-learn.org/stable/ index.html

Metric	DT	KNN	GB	NB	**LDA**	QDA	Dummy	**LOG**	**SGD**
macro-f1	0,497	0,511	0,514	0,514	**0,527**	0,080	0,452	**0,527**	0,481
micro-f1	0,898	0,900	0,918	0,911	0,903	0,083	0,643	0,883	**0,927**

Table 2: TF-IDF sentence classification results.

4.4 Topic Modeling-based Classification of sentences

For the production of the topics and the topic-vectors we used MALLET, a Java framework for various common tasks in NLP, including topic-modeling (McCallum, 2002). Using this tool, we inferred topics over the corpus of the documents in the training set. We subsequently represent firstly the words, and lastly the sentences, of the documents in the training set by their topic-contributions as described in section 3.2. By default, MALLET ignores all 1-letter and 2-letter words. Additionally, we use the NLTK english stop-words list for stop-word filtering [4].

We test the trained topic model by extracting word and sentence-level probabilistic vector representations from the test set. Any word in the test set not present in the training set, is represented as a zero-vector of topic-contributions.

The pipeline for sentence classification using the topics-based approach can be visualized in figure 2 and is outlined below:

- Infer k topics using MALLET's topic model from the training set
- Represent each sentence in the training set using the equation (4).
- Train a classifier on the topics-represented training set
- Represent each sentence in the test set using the trained model from Step 1
- Predict the labels in the represented test set
- Evaluate the classifier using the micro and macro f-measures

5 Results and Discussion

5.1 Classification Results

The experimental results of the classification on the Multiling Dataset, evaluated with the micro-f1 and macro-f1 scores are displayed in tables 2 and 4, for the TF-IDF representation and the topic-based representation, respectively. Baseline results using a simple rule-based classifier (Dummy)

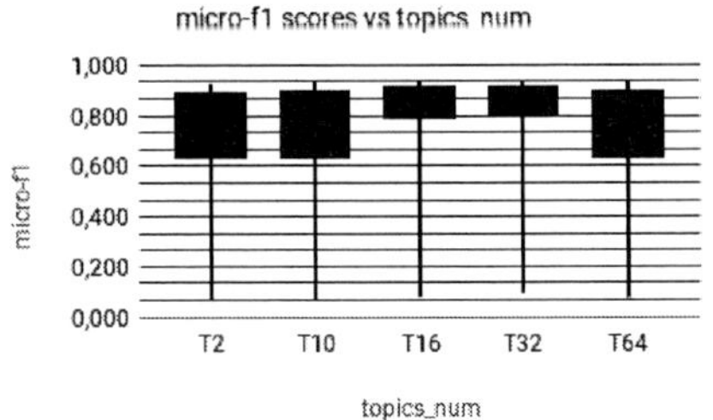

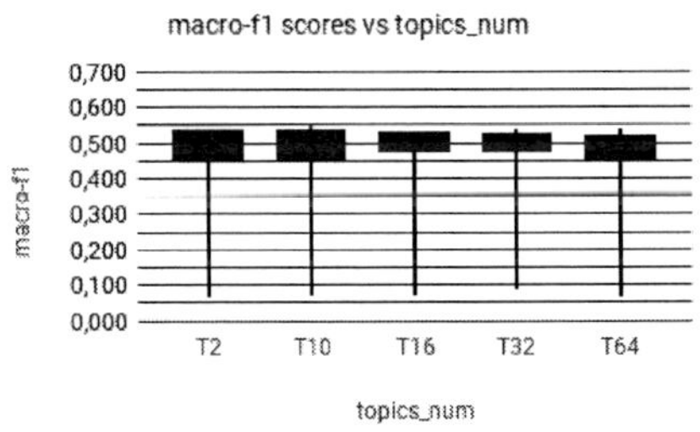

Table 3: Comparison of the micro (top) and macro (bottom) f1 performance of topic modeling, based based on the selection of the number of topics

are also reported, generating predictions with respect to the training set's class distribution – it is thus not influenced by the representation. Dummy gives a micro-f1 score of 0.643 and a macro-f1 score of 0.452.

For TF-IDF, the best macro-f1 score recorded is 0.527 achieved by the Linear Discriminant Analysis (LDA) and Logistic Regression Classifiers (LOG) and the best micro-f1 score is 0.927, given by the Stochastic Gradient Descent Classifier (SGD). TF-IDF achieves significantly better classification results than Dummy , improving micro-f1 by 28% and macro-f1 by 7%, verifying the effectiveness of simple bag-of-word approaches.

For the topic-based representation of sentences, we ran the topic model with a different numbers of topics k on each run, and we trained various classifiers for the task. One major limitation of topic-modeling is that the number of topics needs to be determined experimentally. In order to make an informed decision on k, we examined candi-

---

[4]https://gist.github.com/sebleier/554280

<table>
<tr><td colspan="10" align="center">MICRO F-MEASURE</td></tr>
<tr><td>Topics</td><td>DT</td><td>KNN</td><td>GB</td><td>NB</td><td>LDA</td><td>QDA</td><td>Dummy</td><td>LOG</td><td>SGD</td></tr>
<tr><td>2</td><td>0,885</td><td>0,812</td><td>0,884</td><td>0,922</td><td>0,879</td><td>0,102</td><td>0,643</td><td>0,754</td><td>0,073</td></tr>
<tr><td>10</td><td>0,889</td><td>0,752</td><td>0,895</td><td>0,078</td><td>0,873</td><td>0,175</td><td>0,643</td><td>0,782</td><td>0,927</td></tr>
<tr><td>16</td><td>0,889</td><td>0,802</td><td>0,908</td><td>0,080</td><td>0,884</td><td>0,928</td><td>0,643</td><td>0,800</td><td>0,927</td></tr>
<tr><td>32</td><td>0,894</td><td>0,864</td><td>0,909</td><td>0,093</td><td>0,866</td><td>0,927</td><td>0,643</td><td>0,813</td><td>0,927</td></tr>
<tr><td>64</td><td>0,892</td><td>0,872</td><td>0,916</td><td>0,149</td><td>0,861</td><td>0,927</td><td>0,643</td><td>0,856</td><td>0,073</td></tr>
<tr><td>mean</td><td>0,890</td><td>0,820</td><td>0,902</td><td>0,264</td><td>0,873</td><td>0,612</td><td>0,643</td><td>0,801</td><td>0,585</td></tr>
<tr><td>std</td><td>0,003</td><td>0,044</td><td>0,011</td><td>0,330</td><td>0,008</td><td>0,387</td><td>0,000</td><td>0,034</td><td>0,418</td></tr>
<tr><td colspan="10" align="center">MACRO F-MEASURE</td></tr>
<tr><td>Topics</td><td>DT</td><td>KNN</td><td>GB</td><td>NB</td><td>LDA</td><td>QDA</td><td>Dummy</td><td>LOG</td><td>SGD</td></tr>
<tr><td>2</td><td>0,535</td><td>0,524</td><td>0,535</td><td>0,489</td><td>0,531</td><td>0,101</td><td>0,452</td><td>0,513</td><td>0,068</td></tr>
<tr><td>10</td><td>0,532</td><td>0,506</td><td>0,546</td><td>0,073</td><td>0,535</td><td>0,172</td><td>0,452</td><td>0,520</td><td>0,481</td></tr>
<tr><td>16</td><td>0,528</td><td>0,513</td><td>0,534</td><td>0,076</td><td>0,533</td><td>0,505</td><td>0,452</td><td>0,517</td><td>0,481</td></tr>
<tr><td>32</td><td>0,537</td><td>0,517</td><td>0,531</td><td>0,091</td><td>0,522</td><td>0,481</td><td>0,452</td><td>0,521</td><td>0,481</td></tr>
<tr><td>64</td><td>0,517</td><td>0,512</td><td>0,516</td><td>0,149</td><td>0,539</td><td>0,484</td><td>0,452</td><td>0,527</td><td>0,068</td></tr>
<tr><td>mean</td><td>0,530</td><td>0,514</td><td>0,532</td><td>0,176</td><td>0,532</td><td>0,349</td><td>0,452</td><td>0,520</td><td>0,316</td></tr>
<tr><td>std</td><td>0,007</td><td>0,006</td><td>0,010</td><td>0,159</td><td>0,006</td><td>0,175</td><td>0,000</td><td>0,005</td><td>0,202</td></tr>
</table>

Table 4: Topic modeling results in micro and macro F1 score.

date values for the number of topics, visualized in box-plots presented in table 3. By analyzing table 4 and the box-plots, we concluded that a satisfactory number of topics is 10 for this particular task, as for this k, the Gradient Boosting Classifier (GB) records the highest macro-f1 score. Our decisions are biased towards the macro-f1 instead of the micro-f1 score, since even after the over-sampling of the dataset, the classes are still heavily imbalanced. In addition, we are mostly interested in the sentences that should be included in the summary, which belong to the smaller class. One thing to note, is that as the topic dimension increases, the macro-f1 performance of the Quadratic Discriminant Analysis classifier increases rapidly between Topics 2 and Topics 32 where it reaches a plateau at macro $F1 \approx 0.48$.

Topic-modeling improves on the measures of TF-IDF and Dummy, with a 0.928 micro-f1 score given by the Quadratic Discriminant Analysis (Topics 16) and a 0.546 macro-f1 score given by Gradient Boosting Classifier(Topics 10) resulting in a 3.6% increase in performance, in comparison with the TF-IDF macro-f1 score. The worst-performing classifiers for the selected number of topics are the Naive Bayes (NB) and Quadratic Discriminant Analysis classifiers.

Finally, considering across-topics averages, SGD, QDA and NB appear to be the least stable configurations, while GB, LDA and DT are among the top performers.

5.2 Rouge scores

The rouge scores of the summaries produced by the representation-classifier combinations are displayed in tables 5 and 6. Even though we observed considerable differences in the classification phase between the two representations overall, the final rouge scores are more similar than expected. Bold values correspond to the maximum f-measures for each rouge-metric.

For the TF-IDF, the highest rouge-scores across all classifiers were given by the Quadratic Discriminant Analysis (QDA), while for the Topics-representation, the highest values were recorded by the Naive Bayes Classifier (NB) and Gradient Boosting (GB). The TF-IDF representation results in slightly better rouge-1 to rouge-4 scores while the Topics-based representation produces better rouge-l and rouge-w scores.

6 Conclusions

In this work, we investigated the contribution of topic-based sentence classification to extractive summarization. We examined a variety of configurations for topic modeling by examining a wide range of topics, along with a set of different, diverse classification algorithms. A subsequent large-scale evaluation was performed us-

CLASSIFIER		METRIC					
		rouge-1	rouge-2	rouge-3	rouge-4	rouge-l	rouge-w
KNN	recall	0,226	0,042	0,013	0,007	0,170	0,034
	precision	0,307	0,056	0,017	0,008	0,232	0,127
	f1	0,245	0,046	0,014	0,007	0,186	0,051
LDA	recall	0,127	0,025	0,008	0,003	0,096	0,019
	precision	0,161	0,036	0,017	0,011	0,120	0,065
	f1	0,136	0,027	0,010	0,004	0,103	0,029
GB	recall	0,164	0,032	0,008	0,004	0,132	0,026
	precision	0,258	0,060	0,019	0,013	0,199	0,113
	f1	0,186	0,038	0,010	0,005	0,149	0,040
LOG	recall	0,153	0,031	0,009	0,003	0,115	0,023
	precision	0,184	0,038	0,012	0,006	0,136	0,071
	f1	0,162	0,034	0,010	0,004	0,122	0,034
QDA	recall	0,365	0,106	0,047	0,026	0,264	0,056
	precision	0,364	0,106	0,047	0,027	0,264	0,140
	f1	**0,365**	**0,106**	**0,047**	**0,027**	**0,264**	**0,080**
Dummy	recall	0,344	0,076	0,029	0,014	0,242	0,050
	precision	0,345	0,076	0,028	0,014	0,243	0,125
	f1	0,344	0,076	0,029	0,014	0,242	0,071
NB	recall	0,208	0,034	0,006	0,001	0,148	0,029
	precision	0,232	0,037	0,006	0,001	0,164	0,082
	f1	0,216	0,035	0,006	0,001	0,154	0,042
DT	recall	0,280	0,043	0,010	0,003	0,207	0,041
	precision	0,323	0,045	0,010	0,003	0,239	0,122
	f1	0,292	0,044	0,010	0,003	0,216	0,060
SGD	recall	0,000	0,000	0,000	0,000	0,000	0,000
	precision	0,000	0,000	0,000	0,000	0,000	0,000
	f1	0,000	0,000	0,000	0,000	0,000	0,000

Table 5: TF-IDF Rouge Scores

CLASSIFIER			METRIC				
		rouge-1	rouge-2	rouge-3	rouge-4	rouge-l	rouge-w
KNN	recall	0.326	0.06	0.019	0.01	0.238	0.048
	precsion	0.332	0.062	0.019	0.01	0.241	0.122
	f1	0.328	0.061	0.019	0.01	0.239	0.069
LDA	recall	0.365	0.105	0.046	0.026	0.268	0.057
	precision	0.332	0.063	0.018	0.009	0.236	0.118
	f1	0.327	0.062	0.018	0.009	0.232	0.066
GB	recall	0.334	0.069	0.025	0.015	0.242	0.049
	precision	0.361	0.105	0.046	0.026	0.265	0.14
	f1	0.361	0.104	**0.046**	**0,026**	0.265	0.08
LOG	recall	0.362	0.102	0.045	0.025	0.267	0.056
	precision	0,339	0.069	0.025	0.015	0.245	0.125
	f1	0.336	0.069	0.025	0.015	0.243	0.071
QDA	recall	0.305	0.064	0.022	0.012	0.221	0.045
	precision	0.362	0.101	0.045	0.025	0.267	0.141
	f1	0.361	0.101	0.045	0.025	**0.267**	0.08
Dummy	recall	0.344	0.076	0.029	0.014	0.242	0.05
	precision	0.345	0.076	0.028	0.014	0.243	0.125
	f1	0.344	0.076	0.029	0.014	0.242	0.071
NB	recall	0.313	0.063	0.021	0.013	0.228	0.046
	precision	0.364	0.104	0.046	0.026	0.268	0.142
	f1	**0.364**	**0.104**	0.045	**0.026**	**0.267**	**0.081**
DT	recall	0.303	0.103	0.046	0.023	0.283	0.056
	precision	0.33	0.065	0.022	0.013	0.241	0.125
	f1	0.319	0.064	0.022	0.013	0.232	0.067
SGD	recall	0.323	0.062	0.018	0.009	0.23	0.046
	precision	0.331	0.067	0.022	0.012	0.238	0.124
	f1	0.312	0.065	0.022	0.012	0.226	0.066

Table 6: Topic modeling Rouge Scores

ing micro-f1 and macro-f1 scores. Based on the trained models, we produced summaries for the input documents and we compared them with the ground-truth using several Rouge-metrics. As a baseline, we also implemented a TF-IDF representation of sentences, which follows a traditional bag-of-words weighted approach.

Initial results of this early study show that topic-modeling can be beneficial for sentence classification, as it outperforms the TF-IDF representation, as illustrated by the micro and macro f1 scores in our experiments, albeit this not being the case for the Rouge-based evaluation. We demonstrated that the topics-based approach can easily compete with the TF-IDF approach and shows promise in extractive summarization. Careful task-specific adjustments need to be made however, as the results in the summary evaluation (using Rouge) appear underwhelming compared to those in the classification phase.

In the future, more sophisticated methods such as Principal Component Analysis(PCA) (Jolliffe, 2011) or Linear Semantic Analysis(LSA) (Landauer et al., 1998) can be applied on the presented framework of topics-based sentence representation, in order to project the word-topic vectors into lower-dimensional spaces.

Additionally, more adaptive topic modelling approaches could be applied, removing the need for pre-determined topic specification,(Steyvers and Griffiths, 2017). Moreover, Neural Network classification architectures can be explored, in addition to the set of classifiers we already tested on the dataset. A-priori knowledge on words, phrases and sentences from external sources (e.g. knowledge bases such as Wordnet (A. Miller et al., 1991)) could also prove beneficial for the training phase of the machine-learning models. Finally, future work will take order / target summary length into account, making our results comparable to other systems tackling the Multiling2015 dataset and the state of the art.

References

A. Miller, G., Beckwith, R., Fellbaum, C., Gross, D., and J. Miller, K. (1991). Introduction to WordNet: An On-line Lexical Database*. 3.

Bellman, R. (1958). Dynamic programming and stochastic control processes. *Information and Control*, 1(3):228 – 239.

Blei, D. M. (2012). Probabilistic topic models. *Communications of the ACM*, 55(4):77.

Conroy, J. M., Kubina, J., Rankel, P. A., and Yang, J. S. (2015). *Multilingual Summarization and Evaluation Using Wikipedia Featured Articles*, chapter Chapter 9, pages 281–336.

Genest, P.-E., Lapalme, G., and Yousfi-Monod, M. (2009). Hextac: the creation of a manual extractive run.

Giannakopoulos, G., Kubina, J., Conroy, J., Steinberger, J., Favre, B., Kabadjov, M., Kruschwitz, U., and Poesio, M. (2015). MultiLing 2015: Multilingual Summarization of Single and Multi-Documents, On-line Fora, and Call-center Conversations. In *Proceedings of the 16th Annual Meeting of the Special Interest Group on Discourse and Dialogue*, pages 270–274, Prague, Czech Republic. Association for Computational Linguistics.

Gupta, V. and Lehal, G. S. (2010). A Survey of Text Summarization Extractive Techniques. *Journal of Emerging Technologies in Web Intelligence*, 2(3).

Harris, Z. S. (1954). Distributional Structure. *WORD*, 10(2-3):146–162.

J, J., Pingali, P., Varma, V., J, J., Pingali, P., and Varma, V. (2008). *Sentence Extraction Based Single Document Summarization*.

Jolliffe, I. (2011). Principal Component Analysis. In Lovric, M., editor, *International Encyclopedia of Statistical Science*, pages 1094–1096. Springer Berlin Heidelberg, Berlin, Heidelberg.

Jones, K. S. (2004). A statistical interpretation of term specificity and its application in retrieval. page 9.

Landauer, T. K., Foltz, P. W., and Laham, D. (1998). An introduction to latent semantic analysis. *Discourse Processes*, 25(2-3):259–284.

Lin, C.-Y. (2004). ROUGE: A Package for Automatic Evaluation of Summaries. page 8.

McCallum, A. K. (2002). MALLET: A Machine Learning for Language Toolkit.

Rao, C. and Gudivada, V. (2018). *Computational Analysis and Understanding of Natural Languages: Principles, Methods and Applications*. Handbook of Statistics. Elsevier Science.

Salton, G. and Buckley, C. (1988). Term-weighting approaches in automatic text retrieval. *Information Processing & Management*, 24(5):513–523.

Salton, G., Wong, A., and Yang, C.-S. (1975). A vector space model for automatic indexing. *Communications of the ACM*, 18(11):613–620.

Steyvers, M. and Griffiths, T. (2017). Probabilistic Topic Models. page 15.

Thomas, S., Beutenmüller, C., de la Puente, X., Remus, R., and Bordag, S. (2015). ExB Text Summarizer. In *Proceedings of the 16th Annual Meeting of the Special Interest Group on Discourse and Dialogue*, pages 260–269, Prague, Czech Republic. Association for Computational Linguistics.

Turney, P. D. and Pantel, P. (2010). From Frequency to Meaning: Vector Space Models of Semantics. *Journal of Artificial Intelligence Research*, 37:141–188.

Vicente, M., Alcón, O., and Lloret, E. (2015). The University of Alicante at MultiLing 2015: approach, results and further insights. In *Proceedings of the 16th Annual Meeting of the Special Interest Group on Discourse and Dialogue*, pages 250–259, Prague, Czech Republic. Association for Computational Linguistics.

A Study on Video Game Review Summarization

George Panagiotopoulos
Dpt. of Informatics & Telecommunications
University of Athens
Athens, Greece
sdi1400136@di.uoa.gr

George Giannakopoulos
NCSR Demokritos
Athens, Greece
ggianna@iit.demokritos.gr

Antonios Liapis
Institute of Digital Games
University of Malta
Msida, Malta
antonios.liapis@um.edu.mt

Abstract

Game reviews have constituted a unique means of interaction between players and companies for many years. The dynamics appearing through online publishing have significantly grown the number of comments per game, giving rise to very interesting communities. The growth has, in turn, led to a difficulty in dealing with the volume and varying quality of the comments as a source of information. This work studies whether and how game reviews can be summarized, based on the notions pre-existing in aspect-based summarization and sentiment analysis. The work provides suggested pipeline of analysis, also offering preliminary findings on whether aspects detected in a set of comments can be consistently evaluated by human users.

1 Introduction

The rapid growth of video game industry with new products and technology has significantly increased the popularity of video games. As video games have now become one of the most profitable source of entertainment worldwide, the competition between development companies has increased notably.

Catering for gamers' needs is a demanding task that developers struggle to deal with. Thus, it is crucial for game companies to understand the overall consensus about their products. Additionally, what other people think of a game can also be an important piece of information for potential buyers. Video game reviews offer user-generated data that can be processed in order to identify both people's concerns and user-perceived quality of the game. A number of publishers (Steam[1], GoG[2], etc.) offer a wide range of games, spanning various genres. By visiting such a publisher's store, people are able to look through a game's description and its features, delve into the reviews of the game provided by other users and experts, but also contribute their own review. As some of the games can have millions of reviews, the large scale of information poses the need and challenge of automatic summarization.

The aims of the present paper are:

- to examine if and how aspect-based summarization and sentiment analysis can be applied on the domain of game reviews

- to propose a first approach on game review summarization,

- to offer an evaluation process on the performance of the game review summarization task.

The rest of the paper is structured as follows. In Section 2 we overview the research endeavours related to this work, uniquely positioning it in the current research spectrum and discussing the unique setting of game review summarization. In Section 3, we formulate the problem of game review summarization. In Section 4 we propose

---

[1] https://store.steampowered.com/
[2] https://www.gog.com/games

35

Proceedings of the Multiling 2019 Workshop, co-located with the RANLP 2019 conference, pages 35–43
Varna, Bulgaria, September 6, 2019.
http://doi.org/10.26615/978-954-452-058-8_006

an approach to tackle the problem at hand, while in Section 5 we validate the performance of our method in a user study. We conclude the paper with a summary of the findings and future work, in Section 6.

2 Related Work

The importance of analyzing user reviews has drawn a great deal of interest among researchers. There has been a plethora of studies presenting different approaches on sentiment analysis as well as summarization of user reviews from various domains, such as product reviews and movie reviews. In the following paragraphs we overview such approaches, trying to sketch the research landscape and position this work with respect to other works.

Turney (Turney, 2002) suggests a PMI-based approach for classifying reviews from four different domains (e.g. automobiles, movies, e.t.c) as *recommended* or *not recommended*. His approach consists of three main steps: phrase extraction from a given review by applying POS tagging, orientation estimation for each phrase based on the PMI score between the phrase and the words *excellent* and *poor*, review labelling based on the average orientation of its phrases. In (Hu and Liu, 2004) Hu and Liu present an approach for generating a feature-based opinion summary from a large number of reviews. They propose promising techniques for each stage of their method, which aims at classifying sentences rather than each review as a whole. They present, among others, an iterative algorithm for identifying the underlying sentiment of a word using a small set of seed adjectives combined with WordNet's synset relations (Miller, 1998).

Similarly, Zhuang et al. (Zhuang et al., 2006) propose their approach for producing feature-based summaries on the domain of movie reviews. They make use of regular expressions and Word-Net for feature mining and opinion word identification respectively. POS-tag patterns are used in order to identify feature-opinion pairs. Their experiments produced lower precision and recall scores than the results obtained in the domain of product reviews (Hu and Liu, 2004), mainly because of the peculiarity of movie reviews. Instead of just producing an opinion summary, (Jmal and Faiz, 2013) assess the opinion strength on a product and its features, while exploiting Twitter posts to highlight the most relevant features more effec-

tively. In a more recent work (Rist et al., 2018) identify aspect-based statements from product reviews through patterns extracted from dependency parse trees.

A number of studies have proposed supervised learning approaches by training sentiment classifiers. Pang and Lee (Pang et al., 2002) attempt to classify movie reviews using Naive Bayes, SVM and Max Entropy and multiple feature combinations. Their results indicate that ML techniques on sentiment classification can achieve high accuracy when feature presence instead of feature frequency is used. In (Wilson et al., 2005) the authors attempt to recognize phrase-level contextual polarity by using a two-step process. They firstly classify expressions as polar or neutral and subsequently classify the polar ones as positive, negative or neutral.

A novel flexible summarization framework, called Opinosis, is proposed by Ganesan et al. in (Ganesan et al., 2010). It is a graph-based approach that represents review text as a graph with unique properties and identifies various paths in it, each one acting as a candidate summary. The SMACk system (Dragoni et al., 2018) is an argumentation-based opinion mining framework which detects and extracts aspects coupled with polarities from documents by creating an argumentation graph.

Topic modeling has been widely used as a basis to perform extraction and grouping of aspects. Titov and McDonald (Titov and McDonald, 2008) introduce a Multi-grain LDA model which models global topics and local topics that capture ratable aspects and properties of reviewed items respectively. Their method is particularly suited to aspect extraction from reviews as it does not only identify important terms but also clusters them into coherent groups. In (Lu et al., 2009) aspects in eBay's sellers feedback comments are discovered using PLSA-based techniques. The authors try to group aspect terms that tend to co-occur in comments. Jo and Oh (Jo and Oh, 2011) proposed two generative models to discover aspects and sentiment in reviews. Sentence-level LDA (SLDA) constrains that all words in a single sentence be drawn from one aspect. Aspect and Sentiment Unification Model (ASUM) unifies aspects and sentiment and discovers pairs of aspect, sentiment, which we call senti-aspects.

Recent advances in computing hardware together with the increased availability of data have led to the ubiquitous use of neural networks as an effective tool for producing summaries and identifying sentiment in text.

In (dos Santos and Gatti, 2014) the authors develop a deep convolutional neural network that exploits from character- to sentence-level information to perform sentiment analysis of short texts. Conversely, in (Severyn and Moschitti, 2015) the authors construct a network with just a single convolutional layer and also presented a new model for initializing the weights of the network. A novel deep learning approach to aspect extraction is shown in (Poria et al., 2016) where a 7-layer CNN is combined with linguistic patterns. Using the dataset made available by Pontiki et al. (Pontiki et al., 2016), the authors in (Ruder et al., 2016) propose a hierarchical LSTM-based approach for that task of aspect-based sentiment analysis whilst a Cascaded-CNN architecture is presented in (Wu et al., 2016).

Despite the widespread appeal of video games, there has been little discussion on the domain of game reviews. Yauris and Khodra (Yauris and Khodra, 2017) propose an aspect-based summarization system for Steam reviews. They employ a modified double propagation (DP) algorithm for extracting aspect-sentiment word pairs. Following this, they use a seed list and word similarity to categorize aspect terms into groups, thus producing an aspect-based summary. In (Baowaly et al., 2019) the authors developed a robust model using Gradient Boosting Machine algorithm to predict the Steam review helpfulness.

Most works so far have relied on supervised learning methods by utilizing annotated datasets (Pontiki et al., 2016). As there is currently no existing dataset for aspect-based game review summarization, our work is designed with the aim to minimize the role of supervision. Furthermore, in our undertaking we take into account the following idiosyncrasies of the game setting:

- The folksonomy (dynamic) nature of the terms used in comments. Each genre and possibly game appear to be mapped to specific expectations by its users and, consequently, aspects that the users comment on. There appears that a fixed ontology or aspect set would not be sufficient to describe the aspects of all the game genres that get published over time. This is further accentu-

ated by the fact that hybrid games, combining genres, become a common sight.

- The possible vagueness of aspects, based also on the above comment. We thus examine whether aspects identified through an unsupervised process can be consistently labeled by humans.

- The fact that it is important to hold not a single response of sentiment, but understand the full spectrum of sentiments of players. This means that a single "positive", "negative" or "neutral" answer to how people have commented for an aspect is only a secondary finding. The distribution of comments over these three labels is more interesting and useful, and may be the primary aim of a game review summarization process.

Given the above analysis, we establish a problem definition in the following paragraph, trying to formally frame the game review summarization problem.

3 Problem Definition

As noted, video game reviews are likely to discuss several aspects of the game, such as graphics, gameplay, community e.t.c. Expert/professional reviewers tend to follow specific patterns of summarizing reviews, utilizing the above established aspects. They also provide an overall recommendation and possibly grade, while oftentimes they highlight "pros" and "cons" of the reviewed game. These pros and cons essentially designate the specific, non-formalized, aspects of a game (and possibly of other games of its genre). On the other hand, we should note that the expert reviewers only summarize their own review, which forms a single-document setting. In our case, we examine an approach more suited for a multi-document summarization setting, where several texts (reviews) are to be summarized in a single summary.

To take into account the above "gold standard" human approach, while tackling the multi-document differentiation, we formulate the problem as follows:

Given a set of game reviews $R = \{r_1, r_2, ...\}$ for a game g, the game review summarization task tries to perform the following steps:

aspect identification identify the set A of aspects of the game, that the reviews R comment on.

aspect labeling map each aspect A to a label set $L_A = \{l_1, l_2, ...\}$, where each of l_i is a (possibly weighted) term.

sentiment extraction extract a sentiment distribution S_A of the form $S_A = \{s_{\text{positive}}, s_{\text{neutral}}, s_{\text{negative}}\}$, which describes the user sentiment over each aspect A.

highlight extraction extract the subset $P \in A$ of "pros", where $s_{\text{positive}} > s_{\text{negative}}$ and the subset $C \in A$ of "cons", where $s_{\text{positive}} < s_{\text{negative}}$.

review summary generate a single summary $\mathbb{S}$ containing all the above information.

Within this work we focus on the *aspect identification, aspect labeling* steps. We also touch the *sentiment extraction* and *highlight extraction*, providing baseline implementations. In the following paragraphs, we elaborate on the suggested methods that implement these steps.

4 Proposed Method

In this section we describe in detail the steps of our proposed method. Given a game, we first fetch a set of reviews, which are subsequently split into sentences. After having processed each sentence, we represent them using a bag-of-words (BOW) model. Sentences are then clustered followed by sentiment analysis on each cluster. The individual processing steps are described below :

4.1 Review Representation

Text representation plays a major role in the effectiveness and accuracy of clustering algorithms (Aggarwal and Zhai, 2012). In our approach we represent each review as a set of processed sentences, which are then converted into tf-idf vectors. More precisely, after having segmented each review into sentences, tokenization, stopword removal and lemmatization are applied on each one. For this purpose we employ spaCy v2.0[3], an open-source software library for advanced NLP. Following this, we convert the sentences into tf-idf vectors. Below we provide a review excerpt followed by the extracted sentences:

Global offensive is not the key evolution point that we were hoping for and the response from the

---
[3] https://spacy.io/

Cluster 1	story, character, mode, main, mission
Cluster 2	money, spend, earn, waste, real
Cluster 3	time, fun, long, loading, screen
Cluster 4	reason, ban, permanently, innocent, account
Cluster 5	support, great, bad, community, good

Table 1: Most frequent words in each cluster

community often reflects this view. It is still however a glorious experience that sets a benchmark for all multiplayer shooters.

- global offensive key evolution point hope response community reflect view

- glorious experience set benchmark multiplayer shooter

We also examined whether a word embedding would provide better results. However, the BOW representation method appeared to give more coherent results in the clustering step. It is very likely that the short length of sentences combined with the large vocabulary size has led to this finding. Thus, capturing the context of each sentence via a sentence2vec method can be challenging, probably requiring more specific training data.

4.2 Aspect Extraction

In this step we try to extract the aspects of a game that are mainly discussed by the reviewers. Video game aspects can be either explicitly or implicitly mentioned in a review text. For example, the sentence *"Easily my favorite game with realistic graphics"* clearly expresses an opinion about the aspect *"graphics"*. On the contrary, the sentence *"The grenade explosions are so fake"* does not mention the word *"graphics"* but it obviously refers to the graphics of the game, or possibly the physics engine.

We apply k-means clustering on the previously collected sentences with the aim of producing a cluster-wise summary. The intuition behind this approach is that the produced clusters will exhibit the most salient aspects appearing in the reviews. In Section 5 we elaborate on our decision regarding the number of clusters.

Table 1 lists the most frequent terms appearing in each cluster. As anticipated, the words are semantically close to each other and they seem to represent a specific game aspect. We choose these terms to label the aspect cluster.

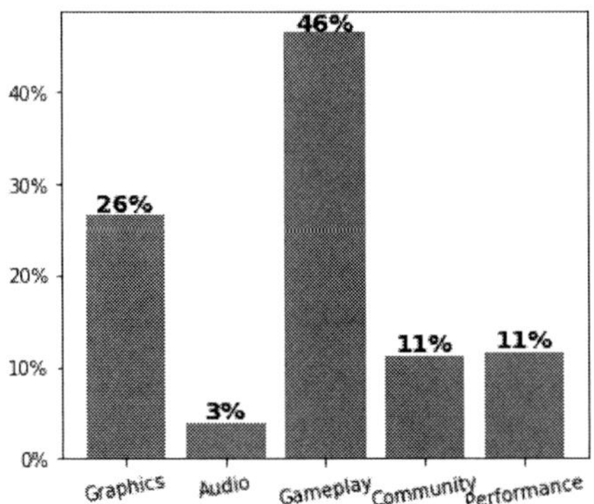

Figure 1: Aspect proportions exhibited in cluster on "The Elder Scrolls V: Skyrim" game

4.3 Aspect Labeling

Another way to label the aspects is to map them to a predefined set of aspect labels, based on gold-standard (i.e. professional) reviews. In Table 2 we show an indicative, human-provided mapping between terms and predefined aspect labels.

Based on the mapping illustrated in Table 2, each sentence can be classified into one of the aspects, by identifying the prevalent aspect of the sentence's words (i.e. terms). For instance, if the majority of the terms in a sentence belong to the *community* aspect, then the sentence is given this label. It should be noted that the term lists needs to be slightly modified based on the game's genre. The reason is that the terms that illustrate the "*gameplay*" aspect of a first-person shooter game differ notably from those of a puzzle or an adventure game. This fact highlights the intricacies of the game review task, where secondary (latent) variables alter the aspect descriptions.

Eventually, we end up with the predefined aspect proportions that each cluster exhibits. In Figure 3 we provide a few indicative sentences from a specific aspect cluster. Then, in Figure 1 we show how the sentences of the cluster led to a distribution over the predefined aspects.

4.4 Sentiment Analysis

The sentiment analysis step focuses on identifying the underlying sentiment that pervades each cluster. Since our clusters consist of sentences we perform sentence-level sentiment analysis.

As there is no sentiment analysis dataset spe-cific to our domain, we decided to use VADER (Hutto and Gilbert, 2014), a lexicon and rule-based sentiment analysis tool that is specifically attuned to sentiments expressed in social media. Interestingly, VADER can tell us how positive, negative and neutral a given sentence is, instead of just classifying the sentence in a single category. VADER combines a dictionary of lexical features to sentiment scores with a set of five heuristics (e.g. punctuation, degree modifiers, e.t.c). Consequently, by calculating the three sentiment scores for each sentence in a cluster and averaging, we can get the distribution of the reviewers' sentiment for this cluster.

4.5 Final Output

The final output of the process is an aspect-based summary of a set of reviews of a specific game, coupled with positive, negative and neutral senti-ment proportions for each aspect. While the initial set of numerous unstructured reviews are consid-erably difficult to deal with, this type of summary enables the reader to retrieve the most relevant information about the game according to his/her need.

5 Experiments

5.1 Experimental Setup

For our experiments we used the Steam review dataset gathered by Zuo (2018). It consists of more than 7 million reviews obtained via Steam's API. Each review text comes with a plethora of features concerning both the game being reviewed and the reviewer. For our experiments, we only utilized the game's ID, the review itself and the number of "helpful" votes the review has received by other community members.

In our experiments, to speedup the clustering process we use only a sample of the reviews of each game consisting of the 10,000 most voted re-views. Due to the syntactical peculiarities found in user-generated reviews, we also had to per-form some extra pre-processing together with the sentence segmentation. This involved repeating phrases and multiple whitespace removal as well as filtering out terms consisting of non-ASCII characters.

Moving on to the clustering process, as reported previously, we decided to use the k-means method. We settled for this method because of the high di-mensionality of our data, making a hierarchical

Graphics	graphic, visual, look, aesthetic, animation, frame
Gameplay	mission, item, map, weapon, mode, multiplayer
Audio	audio, sound, music, soundtrack, melody
Community	community, support, toxic, friendly,
Performance	server, bug, connection, lag, latency, ping, crash, glitch

Table 2: Selected terms for each aspect

```
You get attached to so
many characters and the
world is amazing.

Probably the best open-world
rpg out there.

The vast open world is
absolutely stunning.

If you're looking for a way to
waste massive amounts of time
just trolling around a world
play this.
```

Table 3: Indicative sentences from cluster on "The Elder Scrolls V: Skyrim" game

approach computationally expensive.

Identifying the appropriate number of clusters k can sometimes be one of trickier tasks in the study of clustering. In order to deal with this issue, we attempted to use the elbow method and we also performed Silhouette analysis (Rousseeuw, 1987). Nonetheless, no appreciably optimal k was found by the two methods. However, this is not particularly surprising, in light of the fact that the reviews address a wide range of themes. Thus, the more clusters we create, the higher the coherence will be. Considering, though, that we aim to produce a digestible aspect-based summary using these clusters, it would be irrational to produce too many of them. For this reason, we decided to work with 5 clusters.

5.2 Results

In order to reach a sound conclusion we have performed an empirical evaluation with four different human evaluators. Before describing our evaluation process, we remind the reader that we seek to provide an evaluation process for game review summarization. Given this requirement, we assess the coherence of the generated clusters and examine whether they can be mapped to specific game aspects in a consistent way by humans. This study allows us to understand whether steps of the problem, as formulated in Section 3,

can be evaluated consistently. For the final output of the whole summarization pipeline we expect that standard summary evaluation methods, such as MeMoG (Giannakopoulos and Karkaletsis, 2013) and ROUGE (Lin, 2004) will be useful.

We asked the help of 4 evaluators, who were fluent in the English language. The evaluators were given a set of 20 sentences fetched from each of the five clusters of three different games (for a total of 15 clusters). We also opted for different genres in order to examine the inter-genre differences with respect to the terms used for describing game aspects. They were then asked read each set of sentences and complete the following tasks:

- Select up to n representative sentences from the aspect cluster to represent/summarize the cluster. The idea behind this task is to show whether the cluster was coherent enough to be described by a representative subset of its sentences. The lower the number of representative sentences one would need to use to represent the cluster, the higher the coherence of the cluster.

- Describe the theme of each set using 3 to 5 (possibly multi-word) terms. This task aims to see whether humans can consistently label a given aspect cluster. If so, then the agreed wording(s) can be considered gold-standard, similarly to a Pyramid evaluation (Nenkova and Passonneau, 2004).

- Select one or more predefined terms (gameplay, graphics, audio, community, performance, overall, other) that best describe the aspect, according to the opinion of the human evaluator. We also allowed the user to select "other" as an option, to examine whether a significant number of aspects go beyond the predefined ones. This would indeed indicate the dynamic nature of aspects in the game review summarization setting.

In the "select representative sentences" task, we quantify how many sentences on average were selected by the evaluators to represent the cluster.

ClusterID	Mean	+/- Std. Err
0	9.75	2.14
1	7.00	1.68
2	9.00	2.42
3	7.50	2.02
4	5.25	1.80
5	9.25	2.17
6	5.00	1.73
7	5.75	1.25
8	7.00	1.22
9	4.25	1.60
10	8.50	2.78
11	4.25	1.31
12	5.00	1.08
13	9.00	1.47
14	8.00	2.48

Table 4: Average representative sentences per aspect

We expect that the lower the number, the better the coherence of the cluster. In Table 4 we see, for each cluster, the average number of sentences selected as representative by the users, plus the standard error. We see that, given 20 sentences, the users selected on average from 4 to 9 representative sentences.

In the "describe the theme" task, we examine whether humans can assign consistent labels in an open terminology setting (i.e. without limiting the possible labels). To measure the agreement here we post-processed their terms, semi-automatically creating equivalence classes of terms (which could also have been determined based on an embedding or a linguistic resource). Indicative equivalence classes were:

- ban; ban possible; bans

- best game; best rally game; buy; buy game; buying recommendations; described as best game; ...

- bad community; community; community bad; community sucks; low rank player behaviour bad; toxic community

We then examined, for each cluster, the number of equivalent terms that were used across all evaluators to label the specific aspect cluster. If at least 2 of the 4 evaluators utilize equivalent terms, we consider that the labeling is possible and successful. In all the 15 clusters at least one equivalence class was used consistently. In Figure 2 we show the consistently used equivalence classes per cluster. [4]

---

[4]There are cases where a single evaluator used more than

6 Conclusion

In this paper we discuss the domain of game review summarization. We highlighted main challenges of the domain, showing that a number of unique traits require different approaches from other summarization settings. We formally expressed a view of the task, suggesting a baseline implementation. We then described a possible evaluation process, aiming to quantify the success of the aspect identification and labeling, taking into account coherence and consistent labeling from human evaluators.

This preliminary study of the game review setting opens a number of research questions that we can pursue in the future. First, how does the game genre affect the aspects of a game? Is there a causal relation that connects them? Can we perform automatic evaluation with or without human gold standard summaries? What is different from other summarization settings, concerning the evaluation?

In this work, we offer a first research step towards the emerging and useful domain of game review summarization. We understand that this first step simply highlights interesting points of focus, while providing some intuition on what is meaningful and doable from an evaluation perspective. We feel confident that this will help document and formulate a consistent setting and benchmarking process, helping related endeavors grow in the future.

References

Charu C. Aggarwal and ChengXiang Zhai. 2012. A survey of text clustering algorithms. In *Mining Text Data*.

Mrinal Kanti Baowaly, Yi-Pei Tu, and Kuan-Ta Chen. 2019. Predicting the helpfulness of game reviews: A case study on the Steam store. *Journal of Intelligent & Fuzzy Systems* 36(5):4731–4742.

Cicero dos Santos and Maira Gatti. 2014. Deep Convolutional Neural Networks for Sentiment Analysis of Short Texts. In *Proceedings of COLING 2014, the 25th International Conference on Computational Linguistics: Technical Papers*. Dublin City University and Association for Computational Linguistics, Dublin, Ireland, pages 69–78.

---

one term from an equivalence class, thus leading to counts over 4. However, our counting algorithm ascertains that at least 2 different evaluators will have used a term from the same equivalence class, before increasing the count.

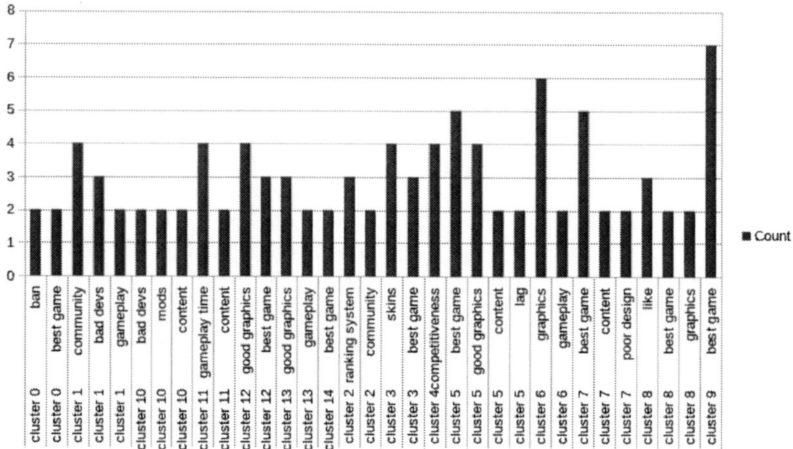

Figure 2: Count of usage for consistent equivalence classes per cluster

Mauro Dragoni, Celia da Costa Pereira, Andrea G. B. Tettamanzi, and Serena Villata. 2018. Combining argumentation and aspect-based opinion mining: The SMACk system. *AI Communications* 31(1):75–95.

Kavita Ganesan, Chengxiang Zhai, and Jiawei Han. 2010. Opinosis: a graphbased approach to abstractive summarization of highly redudant opinions. In *In COLING*.

George Giannakopoulos and Vangelis Karkaletsis. 2013. Summary evaluation: Together we stand npower-ed. In *International Conference on Intelligent Text Processing and Computational Linguistics*. Springer, pages 436–450.

Minqing Hu and Bing Liu. 2004. Mining opinion features in customer reviews. In *AAAI*. volume 4, pages 755–760.

Clayton J Hutto and Eric Gilbert. 2014. Vader: A parsimonious rule-based model for sentiment analysis of social media text. In *Eighth international AAAI conference on weblogs and social media*.

Jihene Jmal and Rim Faiz. 2013. Customer review summarization approach using Twitter and SentiWordNet. In *Proceedings of the 3rd International Conference on Web Intelligence, Mining and Semantics - WIMS '13*. ACM Press, Madrid, Spain, page 1.

Yohan Jo and Alice H. Oh. 2011. Aspect and Sentiment Unification Model for Online Review Analysis. In *Proceedings of the Fourth ACM International Conference on Web Search and Data Mining*. ACM, New York, NY, USA, WSDM '11, pages 815–824. Event-place: Hong Kong, China.

Chin-Yew Lin. 2004. Rouge: A package for automatic evaluation of summaries. In *Text summarization branches out*. pages 74–81.

Yue Lu, ChengXiang Zhai, and Neel Sundaresan. 2009. Rated Aspect Summarization of Short Comments. In *Proceedings of the 18th International Conference on World Wide Web*. ACM, New York, NY, USA, WWW '09, pages 131–140. Event-place: Madrid, Spain.

George Miller. 1998. *WordNet: An electronic lexical database*. MIT press.

Ani Nenkova and Rebecca Passonneau. 2004. Evaluating content selection in summarization: The pyramid method. In *Proceedings of the human language technology conference of the north american chapter of the association for computational linguistics: Hlt-naacl 2004*. pages 145–152.

Bo Pang, Lillian Lee, and Shivakumar Vaithyanathan. 2002. Thumbs up? Sentiment Classification using Machine Learning Techniques. In *Proceedings of the 2002 Conference on Empirical Methods in Natural Language Processing (EMNLP 2002)*.

Maria Pontiki, Dimitris Galanis, Haris Papageorgiou, Ion Androutsopoulos, Suresh Manandhar, Mohammad AL-Smadi, Mahmoud Al-Ayyoub, Yanyan Zhao, Bing Qin, Orphe De Clercq, Vronique Hoste, Marianna Apidianaki, Xavier Tannier, Natalia Loukachevitch, Evgeniy Kotelnikov, Nuria Bel, Salud Mara Jimnez-Zafra, and Glen Eryiit. 2016. SemEval-2016 Task 5: Aspect Based Sentiment Analysis. In *Proceedings of the 10th International Workshop on Semantic Evaluation (SemEval-2016)*. Association for Computational Linguistics, San Diego, California, pages 19–30.

Soujanya Poria, Erik Cambria, and Alexander Gelbukh. 2016. Aspect extraction for opinion mining with a deep convolutional neural network. *Knowledge-Based Systems* 108:42–49.

Michael Rist, Ahmet Aker, and Norbert Fuhr. 2018. Towards Making Sense of Online Reviews Based on

Statement Extraction. In *7th International Conference on Natural Language Processing*. pages 01–12.

Peter Rousseeuw. 1987. Silhouettes: A Graphical Aid to the Interpretation and Validation of Cluster Analysis. *J. Comput. Appl. Math.* 20(1):53–65.

Sebastian Ruder, Parsa Ghaffari, and John G. Breslin. 2016. A Hierarchical Model of Reviews for Aspect-based Sentiment Analysis. *arXiv:1609.02745 [cs]* ArXiv: 1609.02745.

Aliaksei Severyn and Alessandro Moschitti. 2015. Twitter Sentiment Analysis with Deep Convolutional Neural Networks. In *Proceedings of the 38th International ACM SIGIR Conference on Research and Development in Information Retrieval*. ACM, New York, NY, USA, SIGIR '15, pages 959–962. Event-place: Santiago, Chile.

Ivan Titov and Ryan McDonald. 2008. Modeling Online Reviews with Multi-grain Topic Models. *arXiv:0801.1063 [cs]* ArXiv: 0801.1063.

Peter D. Turney. 2002. Thumbs Up or Thumbs Down? Semantic Orientation Applied to Unsupervised Classification of Reviews. *arXiv:cs/0212032* ArXiv: cs/0212032.

Theresa Wilson, Janyce Wiebe, and Paul Hoffmann. 2005. Recognizing Contextual Polarity in Phrase-Level Sentiment Analysis. In *Proceedings of Human Language Technology Conference and Conference on Empirical Methods in Natural Language Processing*.

Haibing Wu, Yiwei Gu, Shangdi Sun, and Xiaodong Gu. 2016. Aspect-based Opinion Summarization with Convolutional Neural Networks. In *2016 International Joint Conference on Neural Networks (IJCNN)*. IEEE, Vancouver, BC, Canada, pages 3157–3163.

K. Yauris and M. L. Khodra. 2017. Aspect-based summarization for game review using double propagation. In *2017 International Conference on Advanced Informatics, Concepts, Theory, and Applications (ICAICTA)*. pages 1–6.

Li Zhuang, Feng Jing, and Xiao-Yan Zhu. 2006. Movie Review Mining and Summarization. In *Proceedings of the 15th ACM International Conference on Information and Knowledge Management*. ACM, New York, NY, USA, CIKM '06, pages 43–50.

Zhen Zuo. 2018. Sentiment Analysis of Steam Review Datasets using Naive Bayes and Decision Tree Classifier. Technical report, University of Illinois at UrbanaChampaign.

Social Web Observatory: An entity-driven, holistic information summarization platform across sources

Leonidas Tsekouras, Georgios Petasis
Institute of Informatics and Telecommunications
N.C.S.R. Demokritos
Greece
{ltsekouras,petasis}@iit.demokritos.gr

Aris Kosmopoulos
SciFY PNPC
TEPA Lefkippos - NCSR Demokritos
27, Neapoleos, 153 41 Ag. Paraskevi, Greece
akosmo@scify.org

Abstract

The Social Web Observatory is an entity-driven, sentiment-aware, event summarization web platform, combining various methods and tools to overview trends across social media and news sources in Greek. SWO crawls, clusters and summarizes information following an entity-centric view of text streams, allowing to monitor the public sentiment towards a specific person, organization or other entity. In this paper, we overview the platform, outline the analysis pipeline, focusing on the article clustering and title extraction aspects. We then perform a user study aimed to quantify the usefulness of the system and especially the meaningfulness and coherence of discovered events in a Greek language setting, getting promising results.

1 Introduction

Entity-driven event detection and summarization is needed in real-life scenarios, such as due diligence, risk assessment, fraud detection, etc.; where the entities are usually firms or individuals.

The *Social Web Observatory* is an initiative that aims to help researchers interested in the social sciences and digital humanities study how information spreads in the news and other user-generated content, such as social media posts and comments. The overall system is composed of a back-end and a web application that provides a friendly front-end to the final users.

In this work we overview Social Web Observatory and we examine, through a human user study, a set of research questions related to its summarization performance:

- Are the event clusters created by the system meaningful, reflecting a single event?

- How well does the system avoid bringing irrelevant articles into the clusters?

- Does the system choose representative titles for the identified events?

The rest of the paper is structured as follows. In Section 2 we outline some related work and position our work. Then, in Sections 3 and 4 we describe the platform, designate the problem it is meant to face and outline the methods used in the Social Web Observatory analysis pipeline. We continue, in Section 5, by describing the experiments conducted to answer our research questions, which we then discuss in Section 6. We conclude the paper in Section 7.

2 Related Work

Our event detection is based on clustering the news articles that are found to be related to a given entity. Each cluster that results from the clustering, is considered an event. The clustering algorithm we used is agglomerative hierarchical clustering and for the similarity measure we used n-gram graphs by (Giannakopoulos and Karkaletsis, 2009), which can capture the order of n-grams in an article, taking also into account the frequency of their co-occurrence within a window. This similarity falls under the string-based measures as defined by (Gomaa and Fahmy, 2013) in their survey of text similarity measures, which means it operates on the characters of the text and does not use any external or semantic information.

Event detection can be useful for emergencies such as natural disasters, as detecting events on social media posts can give us information that may not be easily available elsewhere in order to plan the response to the emergency more effec-

Proceedings of the Multiling 2019 Workshop, co-located with the RANLP 2019 conference, pages 44–52
Varna, Bulgaria, September 6, 2019.
http://doi.org/10.26615/978-954-452-058-8_007

tively. Event detection can also help when inspecting past events. In our case we are interested in extracting events from several documents to examine what happened that is related to a specific entity. Knowing that an event happened at some specific time can help the user build a conclusion about the sentiment for the entity at that time, or why it changed. Also, using multiple documents which contain mentions of the entity for describing an event can help to further clarify its type (e.g. if an employee "left" the company to go home or was fired) and what actually happened (Hong et al., 2011).

Because of its usefulness, a lot of work has been done on event detection for textual data. For social media posts the latest works work even for real-time scenarios (Hasan et al., 2018), and as (Imran et al., 2018) note, there are additional challenges such as the latency requirements and the informal language used on such platforms.

However, we do not have to tackle these challenges, as we focus on news articles which should use more formal language and the detection is not time sensitive. There is already a delay from when the event happens to when it is reported on news websites and we can detect it on a later time to display on our application. Our focus is more in the quality of the detected events.

Neural networks have been used with success for event detection and even language-agnostic models have been developed such as (Feng et al., 2018), who tested their network on English, Spanish and Chinese.

Litvak et al. (2016) extract events from Twitter by clustering them with the EDCoW method (Weng and Lee, 2011) which they extend to improve the detection of events that unfold at the same time, a case where the wavelet analysis of EDCoW couldn't differentiate the two separate events. The user can see the top tweets, hashtags and words as a summary of the event, similar to our case, as well as a textual summary with sentences extracted from texts found in the links of the tweets that the cluster contains. There is also an interactive map with the sentiment of each country for the event.

Toda and Kataoka (2005) use document clustering based on Named Entities to tackle the problem of document retrieval for search results. They employ NER to find the important term candidates of the documents and create an index of the terms they select using two proposed criteria. Finally they categorize these terms in order to form clusters of documents. The evaluation was done on news articles, as in our case, and the results showed that users liked the categorization of the results by the Named Entities, however the authors didn't evaluate the clustering part of the system at that time.

Montalvo et al. (2015) proposed an agglomerative clustering algorithm that uses only information about the Named Entities in order to create clusters of news articles talking about the same, specific event, that can work in a bilingual setting. Other than the bilingual nature of their documents, the task is similar to our case. The existence of the same entity in the articles as well as the entity's category are both used to perform the clustering. Their results are very encouraging, and outperformed state-of-the-art algorithms.

There is also an approach by (Tsekouras et al., 2017) where the authors used just the named entities and optionally some of the more unique terms of news articles in order to cluster them into events using the k-means algorithm with a similarity matrix generated by comparing the texts with n-gram graphs. The results show that using just the named entities can make the creation of the graphs significantly faster while achieving the same or better performance than using the full text, especially on multilingual corpora.

While (Beineke et al., 2004) have defined "sentiment summarization" as selecting part of the text that best conveys the author's opinion, we consider it as creating a summary from a number of texts that talk about a specific topic while keeping the overall sentiment intact. Using the sentiment while making a summary of the documents is important, because as (Lerman et al., 2009) have found, users prefer summaries that come from sentiment-aware summarizers.

In this paper, we describe a tool that brings entity-centric, sentiment-aware, multi-document information summarization as a tool. The tool integrates a variety of intermediate analyses to fulfil its purpose, providing a unique combination of features that empower social scientists and researchers to identify and follow public trends and stances, specifically targeted to user selected entities. In the following section we overview the platform and the technologies behind it.

3 Platform Overview

The Social Web Observatory is an initiative aiming to help researchers (mainly of the social sciences and digital humanities) and journalists to study information diffusion in the social web (news and user generated content - such as comments and posts in social media networks). The Social Web Observatory listens a wide variety of news sources (more than 2000 RSS sources which post multiple news articles daily) and user generated content (such as comments in DISQUS and tweets in Twitter). Content is indexed through a search infrastructure, enabling users to retrieve context through sets of keywords, for further analysis. Content retrieved through keyword search is analysed along various dimensions to extract indicators such as trends, coverage, events, sentiment, stance, etc. Both context and indicators are visualised through predefined dashboards and other analytics tools, to provide information and insights on the various issues defined by keyword searches.

The Social Web Observatory web application allows users to create an account and define entities with public or private access, for which dashboards are created. Each entity is comprised of a title, a type (which may allow the user to add additional fields, such as first, middle and last name) and some optional fields such as their social media information and URLs for the entity's web, Wikipedia and Wikidata pages. The user can also specify keywords to include in the search for the entity, such as alternative names or nicknames that people use to refer to the entity and keywords to exclude from the search, which can be useful if for example a last name of an entity is also a word in that language. An entity being "public" means that all users of the application can view the dashboard for that entity (but only the owner can edit it), while "private" means that only the creator of the entity is aware of its existence and can see its dashboard or edit it. A screenshot of the entity creation screen of the application can be seen in Figure 1.

The dashboard of an entity tries to show an overview of what is being said related to the entity on the web over a given date range, which the user can change. It contains information such as how many articles, comments and tweets related to that entity have been collected over the selected time period and how many unique domains had articles and comments about the entity. Then there

Figure 1: Part of the entity creation screen of the web application.

are tabs for more specific information about the news articles, comments and tweets about the entity, which contain a number of charts. The "sentiment over time" chart shows how the number of positive, neutral and negative documents (whose type depends on the selected tab) changes over the selected time period. For news articles, we also display the automatically detected events on the chart. The user can click an event to reveal more information about it. The user can also click a point on the chart to reveal the titles of the documents that correspond to that time point and view them at their source web page. Each of the articles, comments and tweets tabs also contain a graph that shows how many of the total collected items in each case were found to contain the entity over the same time period. This shows how much of the web is concerned with that entity at a given time.

The back-end gathers news articles from a variety of RSS sources, crawls some of the news websites to gather comments for their articles or through DISQUS, and receives tweets from Twitter. These news articles, comments and tweets are all analyzed to identify any entities that they contain, obtain their overall sentiment as well as the sentiment for each of the mentioned entities. Finally the news articles are clustered in order to form events. Since we perform named entity recognition (NER) on the articles from which the events are formed, each event can be linked to the entities that are mentioned in the articles that it contains.

4 Proposed System

The research problem which the SWO platform faces is the following. Given

- a set of text streams $\mathbb{S}$,

- a set of surface representations (i.e. alternative wordings) of an entity $\mathbb{E}$,

- a time span $\mathbb{T}$,

we are called to provide a list $\mathbb{L}$ of events, published within the time span $\mathbb{T}$, referring to the entity $\mathbb{E}$ and annotated by the sentiment expressed therein. The events should ideally be identified by a representative title and should be mapped to (i.e. supported/explained by) a number of texts from the input text streams $\mathbb{S}$. To face this problem, the Social Web Observatory project combines a number of approaches into an analysis pipeline, as described below.

The pipeline for the creation of events from the news articles is supported by the Elasticsearch (Gormley and Tong, 2015) database and begins with the news gathering. This is done through crawling a custom list of over 2000 RSS feeds one by one, receiving the available news articles from each feed and adding the ones that we don't already have to the Elasticsearch index where we keep all the articles. This process is run every 20 minutes on our server.

Periodically, we run the next step of the pipeline, entity detection and aspect-based and document-level sentiment analysis (Petasis et al., 2014; Papachristopoulos et al., 2018). This begins by taking as input the latest raw news articles/comments/tweets from the gathering step, processing and saving them in another index where we keep the processed news articles. The processing starts by detecting any entities that are in the text. For this purpose, the keywords provided by users are primarily used (for direct matching), in cooperation with an automated NER system (OpinionBuster (Petasis et al., 2014)) for some predefined types of entities, such as persons. News articles that contain entity mentions are kept for further processing. Then, the overall sentiment of each textual artifact is found as well as the sentiment for each of the entity mentions that were found in the text. For sentiment analysis, OpinionBuster (Petasis et al., 2014), a state-of-the-art system for the Greek language is being used. OpinionBuster employs a rule-based approach for performing polarity detection, based on compositional polarity classification (Klenner et al., 2009). It analyses the input texts with the aid of a polarity lexicon that specifies the prior polarity of words, which contains more than 360,000 unique word forms (Greek is an inflectional language) and more than 35,000 phrases. As a second

step, the latest versions of Ellogon's (Petasis et al., 2002) dependency parser and chunker are used to determine dependencies and phrases that are the basis for a compositional treatment of phrase-level polarity assignment. Once polarity has been detected, it is distributed over the involved entity mentions with the help of dependencies originating from verbs, in order to distinguish whether the entity mentions receive or generate the polarity detected in the phrases. In case, however, a verb is encountered that cannot be handled by a rule then a simple heuristic is applied, which assigns the detected polarity to all entity mentions within the phrase. At the end of the sentiment analysis step, we have articles, comments, and tweets with the entities that they mention, the overall sentiment and the sentiment for each of the entities (calculated by summing the sentiment for each of the entity's occurences).

The last step is clustering the news articles into events. The input for this step is the processed articles, and the output the clusters, each of which represents an event. The events are saved in another Elasticsearch index that is read by the web application in order to display the events to the user. We assume that most news events should happen at daytime, so we run the clustering on the articles of each day individually. This means that if an event starts in one day and ends the next, we might miss or cluster it as two separate events. The clustering service starts the clustering for each day when that day has passed and all articles that were gathered within that day are processed by the previous step.

The clustering uses n gram graphs (Giannakopoulos and Karkaletsis, 2009) to create a representation of each news article, which are then compared with each other in order to calculate the similarity matrix between all the texts. The news items are clustered using a modified version of the NewSum (Giannakopoulos et al., 2014) clustering algorithm. The original NewSum clustering represented each text with an n-gram graph and grouped together documents that surpassed a heuristically-defined threshold of similarity (specifically Normalized Value Similarity, which takes into account the overlap between graph edges and their relative weights (Giannakopoulos and Karkaletsis, 2009)). Thus, if a the similarity sim of a text a to a text b exceeds the threshold T, then: $\{a, b\} \in C$, where C is a cluster (i.e. set of texts). The caveat was that in several cases a was marginally, but sufficiently similar to b, which in turn was marginally, but sufficiently similar to a text c. This meant that a, b, c would belong to the same cluster C, even though a and c had almost nothing in common. Essentially, the algorithm did not enforce coherence across all pairs within the same cluster.

In the SWO version of the algorithm an agglomerative hierarchical clustering algorithm which ascertains a minimum coherence (i.e. variation of similarity) across all pairs within a cluster was employed to produce clusters of articles. Essentially, the hierarchical clustering only adds articles to a cluster, if they have sufficient similarity to all cluster articles. This causes smaller, more coherent clusters, and prefers precision (keeping clusters clean) over recall (bringing in the maximum number of related news).

The system also extracts a title selected from the articles contained in the cluster, following a centroid-based approach: after representing all the article titles as a bag-of-words in a vector space, the system chooses the title which is closest to the centroid of all the article titles in this space.

Thus, through the clustering process, the clusters have a title and the IDs of the news articles which they contain. After the clustering runs, we need to find out which entities are related to each cluster (event) so we can later filter them by their entities. This will allow us to show only the events that are relevant to an entity in its dashboard page. To do that, we get the unique article IDs from all the clusters that were produced, retrieve them from the processed news articles index, and for each cluster we gather all the entities from all its articles and save them together with the other information about the cluster to the events Elasticsearch index.

The events then can finally be viewed on the web application in the "sentiment over time" chart of an entity's dashboard, as shown in Figure 2. Each colored plot band on the chart represents an event, starting and ending at the first and last publication times of its articles respectively. The chart shows the 50 largest events in the selected time period measured by the number of articles they contain (cluster size). By clicking on an event, the user is shown its title, start and ending times, as well as the sentiment distribution of the event's articles (i.e. how many positive, neutral and negative articles are in the event). The navigator control at the bottom of the chart helps the user click events with very small timespans by allowing them to zoom in.

5 Experiments

In order to evaluate if the events we create are coherent and if they can be labeled consistently by different humans, we ran a user study with three annotators. The annotators (Greek natives) were shown the title and articles of each event in Greek and were asked three questions each time:

- Do the articles of the cluster appear to represent a single event? (Yes/No)

- How many articles do they feel are irrelevant to others? (Number between 0 and the total articles of the cluster)

- Does the cluster (event) title reflect the event well? (Badly/Barely Acceptably/Well enough)

The data we used were the 30 events that contained the most news articles in the time period between July 1 and July 14 of 2019. This data, containing the event titles, date ranges and their articles with publication date, sentiment analysis/NER results and text content is available upon request.

With the answers of the annotators, we can then run statistical tests in order to see the inter-annotator agreement, as well as how the event clustering performs.

For the inter-annotator agreement we ran two different tests. First, we ran paired t-tests between all annotator pairs for the number of articles that they found irrelevant in the events, in order to see if there is a statistically significant difference between their answers. We also ran a chi-squared test with the two categorical variables being the annotator ID and their answers on whether they felt that the cluster's articles represented a single event. This test will show us whether there is a dependence of the result (answer) and the annotator, or whether the annotators seem to provide similar answers.

To see if the clusters are coherent, we studied how many irrelevant articles were found in each cluster by the annotators as a percentage of the cluster size and also the cluster size distribution, to support the cluster coherence result.

6 Results

In this section we will present the results of the described experiments for each set of experiments,

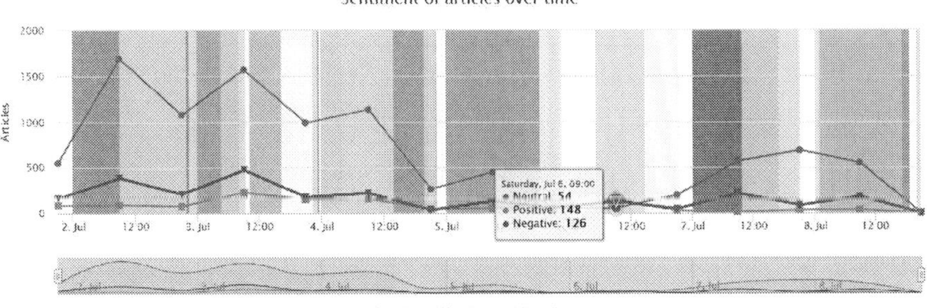

Figure 2: The "sentiment over time" chart for articles, with the colored bands representing events.

indicating how they answer our original research questions posed in Section 1.

Essentially, we examined the event cluster coherence (first two questions) and the title assignment quality (third question). Below, we describe how we ascertained that the study was meaningful and the results we got.

6.1 Inter-annotator Agreement

Our first challenge is to show that annotators can consistently judge the system. We first performed a chi-squared test to show if the annotators agree on whether each cluster represents a single event, the results show that there is no statistically significant dependence between the annotator and the resulting answer for the question (p-value = 0.81). Therefore, we can say that the annotator's answers are independent from the individual annotators, that is, the events seem to get the same answer regardless of who is the annotator.

We, also, performed a set of paired t-tests between the annotators to show whether the distributions of errors (irrelevant articles) identified by each annotator on each event were different. The tests showed that there is no statistically significant difference between any pair of annotators (all p-values are > 10%, see Table 1). This means that the annotators seem to agree on how many articles are irrelevant in each cluster, which indicates a consistent evaluation process.

Given the above findings, we can consider the evaluation task meaningful enough to provide useful feedback.

6.2 Clustering Coherence

To analyze the coherence of the clusters, we made two plots. The first one (Figure 3) shows the cluster coherence according to our annotators, mean-

Annotator Pair	p-value
A & B	0.1033
B & C	0.3256
A & C	0.4235

Table 1: p-values of paired t-tests between the three annotators.

ing how frequently we find clusters with a certain percent of irrelevant articles, according to the annotators' judgement. We see that in over 90% of the clusters the percentage of irrelevant articles that are contained in the cluster was perceived to be less than 10%. There is a very small percentage of clusters (around 2%) where the irrelevant articles make up 10-20% of the cluster. Around 5% of the clusters contain around 30-40% irrelevant articles. There are some more clusters that have around 60-70% irrelevant articles in them, but that is also a very small amount (around 2%). This shows that, overall, most clusters have a very low amount of irrelevant articles in them. At this point we should note that high percentages of irrelevant articles within clusters could also be attributed to small clusters, where a single error could amount to a big percentage of error (our error analysis indicated that this was the case).

We next studied the cluster size distribution to better understand if the clusters were also useful (i.e. non-trivial, having only 1 article). For each cluster size (article count contained), we see how many clusters of that size exist in our evaluated data. Looking at the cluster size statistical summary (quartiles) in Table 2, we see that the minimum number of articles found in any cluster is 3. Combining this with Figure 4, we observe that almost half of the clusters are small, but non-trivial,

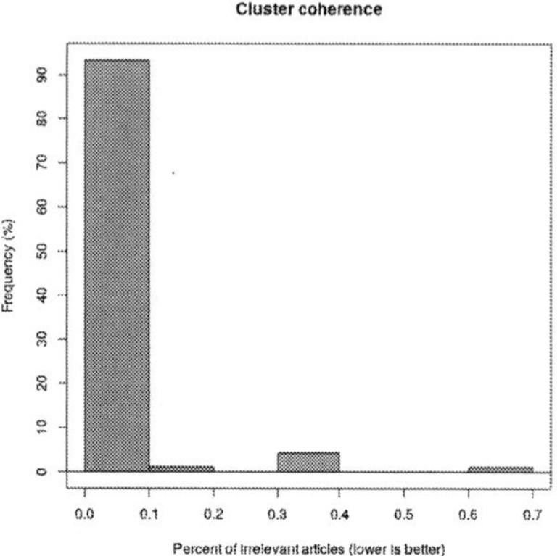

Figure 3: Clustering coherence according to the annotators.

Min	1st Qu.	Median	3rd Qu.	Max
3	3	5	7,75	26

Table 2: Basic statistical summary of cluster sizes.

meaning they contain 3-5 articles. The other half has over 5 articles (the median is 5 articles), in some cases even containing more than 20. Therefore, we can draw the conclusion that the clusters seem to be coherent, meaningful and useful.

We have to note that this evaluation takes into account only the precision of the clustering, as we cannot draw any conclusions about the recall. However, previous works (Giannakopoulos et al., 2014) have suggested that having better precision in such a task gives more perceived value for the user than recall. That is, users prefer small, clean clusters than larger clusters which may contain more of the relevant articles but also more off-

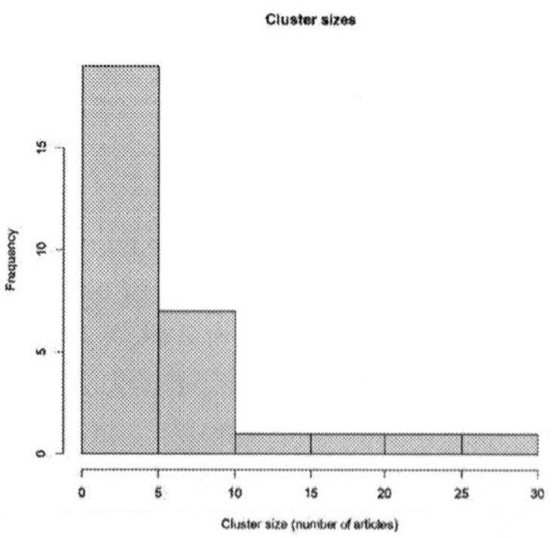

Figure 4: Cluster size distribution.

topic articles.

We also measured the average perceived appropriateness of a title for a given cluster, by assigning the value 0 to "badly", 1 to "barely acceptably" and 2 to "well enough". In our data, in 23 of the 30 events (76% of the cases) the quality was at least 1 on average. In 50% of the overall events the title was considered good enough. Thus, the users seem to be able to understand what events are about from their title.

In the final section of this work we summarize what we did and suggest future steps.

7 Conclusion

In this work, we presented Social Web Observatory, an initiative that aims to show how information is diffused and spread in the social web, via a web application and a back-end system which analyzes the gathered data. Part of this system is using event detection to show events to the user, in order to help them explain why the sentiment about an entity may have changed at a given time. The event detection is run on the news articles of each day, which are analyzed for sentiment and entity recognition. On the user study that we performed, the annotators seemed to agree that the clusters contained very little irrelevant articles, which means the overall pipeline is suitable for our use case. Furthermore, we saw that the title extracted and assigned to each event is in more than 75% of the cases at least acceptable.

As future work, we want to improve the scalability of the overall pipeline to allow it to run on a larger amount of articles, as we continue to increase the number of RSS feeds that we monitor over time. Because we run the event detection periodically (once per day), in this work we were not concerned with its speed, so there is room for improvement in that area. For example we could employ blocking techniques as they have shown to significantly improve the scalability of document clustering in (Pittaras et al., 2018) without hurting the performance too much.

Acknowledgments

We acknowledge support of this work by the project "APOLLONIS: Greek Infrastructure for Digital Arts, Humanities and Language Research and Innovation" (MIS 5002738) which is implemented under the Action "Reinforcement of the Research and Innovation Infrastructure", funded by the Operational Programme "Competitiveness, Entrepreneurship and Innovation" (NSRF 2014-2020) and co-financed by Greece and the European Union (European Regional Development Fund).

References

Philip Beineke, Trevor Hastie, Christopher Manning, and Shivakumar Vaithyanathan. 2004. Exploring sentiment summarization. In *Proceedings of the AAAI spring symposium on exploring attitude and affect in text: theories and applications*. The AAAI Press Palo Alto, CA, volume 39.

Xiaocheng Feng, Bing Qin, and Ting Liu. 2018. A language-independent neural network for event detection. *Science China Information Sciences* 61(9). https://doi.org/10.1007/s11432-017-9359-x.

George Giannakopoulos and Vangelis Karkaletsis. 2009. N-gram graphs: Representing documents and document sets in summary system evaluation. In *Proceedings of Text Analysis Conference TAC2009 (To appear)*.

George Giannakopoulos, George Kiomourtzis, and Vangelis Karkaletsis. 2014. Newsum:"n-gram graph"-based summarization in the real world. In *Innovative Document Summarization Techniques: Revolutionizing Knowledge Understanding*. IGI Global, pages 205–230.

Wael H Gomaa and Aly A Fahmy. 2013. A survey of text similarity approaches. *International Journal of Computer Applications* 68(13):13–18.

Clinton Gormley and Zachary Tong. 2015. *Elasticsearch: the definitive guide: a distributed real-time search and analytics engine*. " O'Reilly Media, Inc.".

Mahmud Hasan, Mehmet A Orgun, and Rolf Schwitter. 2018. A survey on real-time event detection from the Twitter data stream. *Journal of Information Science* 44(4):443–463. https://doi.org/10.1177/0165551517698564.

Yu Hong, Jianfeng Zhang, Bin Ma, Jianmin Yao, Guodong Zhou, and Qiaoming Zhu. 2011. Using cross-entity inference to improve event extraction. In *Proceedings of the 49th Annual Meeting of the Association for Computational Linguistics: Human Language Technologies-Volume 1*. Association for Computational Linguistics, pages 1127–1136.

Muhammad Imran, Carlos Castillo, Fernando Diaz, and Sarah Vieweg. 2018. Processing Social Media Messages in Mass Emergency: Survey Summary. In *Companion of the The Web Conference 2018 on The Web Conference 2018 - WWW '18*. ACM Press, Lyon, France, pages 507–511. https://doi.org/10.1145/3184558.3186242.

Manfred Klenner, Stefanos Petrakis, and Angela Fahrni. 2009. Robust compositional polarity classification. In *Proceedings of the International Conference RANLP-2009*. Association for Computational Linguistics, Borovets, Bulgaria, pages 180–184. http://www.aclweb.org/anthology/R09-1034.

Kevin Lerman, Sasha Blair-Goldensohn, and Ryan McDonald. 2009. Sentiment summarization: evaluating and learning user preferences. In *Proceedings of the 12th Conference of the European Chapter of the Association for Computational Linguistics on - EACL '09*. Association for Computational Linguistics, Athens, Greece, pages 514–522. https://doi.org/10.3115/1609067.1609124.

Marina Litvak, Natalia Vanetik, Efi Levi, and Michael Roistacher. 2016. Whats up on twitter? catch up with twist! In *Proceedings of COLING 2016, the 26th International Conference on Computational Linguistics: System Demonstrations*. pages 213–217.

Soto Montalvo, Raquel Martnez, Vctor Fresno, and Agustn Delgado. 2015. Exploiting named entities for bilingual news clustering: Exploiting Named Entities for Bilingual News Clustering. *Journal of the Association for Information Science and Technology* 66(2):363–376. https://doi.org/10.1002/asi.23175.

Leonidas Papachristopoulos, Pantelis Ampatzoglou, Ioanna Seferli, Andriani Zafeiropoulou, and Georgios Petasis. 2018. Introducing sentiment analysis for the evaluation of library's services effectiveness. In *Proceedings of the 10th Qualitative and Quantitative Methods in Libraries International Conference (QQML2018)*. Chania, Greece.

Georgios Petasis, Vangelis Karkaletsis, Georgios Paliouras, Ion Androutsopoulos, and Constantine D. Spyropoulos. 2002. Ellogon: A New Text Engineering Platform. In *Proceedings of the 3rd International Conference on Language Resources and Evaluation (LREC 2002)*. European Language Resources Association, Las Palmas, Canary Islands, Spain, pages 72–78. http://www.ellogon.org/petasis/bibliography/LREC2002/LREC2002petasis.pdf.

Georgios Petasis, Dimitris Spiliotopoulos, Nikos Tsirakis, and Panayotis Tsantilas. 2014. Sentiment analysis for reputation management: Mining the greek web. In Aristidis Likas, Konstantinos Blekas, and Dimitris Kalles, editors, *Artificial Intelligence: Methods and Applications - 8th Hellenic Conference on AI, SETN 2014, Ioannina, Greece, May 15-17, 2014. Proceedings*. Springer, volume 8445 of *Lecture Notes in Computer Science*, pages 327–340.

Nikiforos Pittaras, George Giannakopoulos, Leonidas Tsekouras, and Iraklis Varlamis. 2018. Document clustering as a record linkage problem. In *Proceedings of the ACM Symposium on Document Engineering 2018*. ACM, page 39.

Hiroyuki Toda and Ryoji Kataoka. 2005. A search result clustering method using informatively named entities. In *Proceedings of the 7th annual ACM international workshop on Web information and data management*. ACM, pages 81–86.

Leonidas Tsekouras, Iraklis Varlamis, and George Giannakopoulos. 2017. A graph-based text similarity measure that employs named entity information. In *RANLP*. pages 765–771.

Jianshu Weng and Bu-Sung Lee. 2011. Event detection in twitter. In *Fifth international AAAI conference on weblogs and social media*.

EASY-M: Evaluation System for Multilingual Summarizers

Marina Litvak, Natalia Vanetik and Yael Veksler
Department of Software Engineering
Shamoon Engineering College
Beer Sheva, Israel
{marinal, natalyav, yaelva}@sce.ac.il

Abstract

Automatic *text summarization* aims at producing a shorter version of a document (or a document set). Evaluation of summarization quality is a challenging task. Because human evaluations are expensive and evaluators often disagree between themselves, many researchers prefer to evaluate their systems automatically, with help of software tools. Such a tool usually requires a point of reference in the form of one or more human-written summaries for each text in the corpus. Then, a system-generated summary is compared to one or more human-written summaries, according to selected measures (also called *metrics*). However, a single metric cannot reflect all quality-related aspects of a summary. In this paper we present the EvAluation SYstem for Multilingual Summarization (EASY-M), which enables the evaluation of system-generated summaries in 23 languages with several quality measures, based on comparison with their human-generated counterparts. The system also provides comparative results with two built-in baselines. The EASY-M system is freely available for the NLP community[1].

1 Introduction

Automatic *text summarization* aims at representing a text document or a document set in a short concise form, called a *summary*. The size of a summary is usually limited by a user-defined number of words, sentences, or percentage of the orig-

inal text. A summary can be either generic or tailored to fit the user's needs. The former is expected to convey the meaning of the whole text while the latter should reflect the interests of a user. Expressions of the user's interests can come in many forms, including those of query, subject, and style. Several extensive surveys of automatic summarization can be found in (Nenkova et al., 2011; Nenkova and McKeown, 2012; Das and Martins, 2007; Llorct and Palomar, 2012).

Automatic text summarization approaches can be divided into two main categories. *Extractive summarization* (Gupta and Lehal, 2010; Gambhir and Gupta, 2017) deals with selecting a subset of sentences from the original document(s) without modifying them. *Abstractive summarization* can compile summaries by extracting parts of original sentences (this approach is known as compressive summarization (Gambhir and Gupta, 2017)), or by generating new, original sentences. (Kasture et al., 2014)

The need for quality assessment of summarization tools is obvious. Using human evaluators is extremely time-consuming and labor-intensive. Additional issues arise when using this approach, such as the qualification of evaluators and their agreement on a content of generated summaries. (Pittaras et al., 2019) Also, hiring qualified evaluators to work with summaries in multiple languages is not an easy and often tedious task. Therefore, there is an existing need to construct automatic summary evaluation tools that provide consistent results for multiple languages. Moreover, these tools must provide a wide range of metrics for covering multiple aspects of summary quality, such as the informativeness, coverage of the main topics of a document, and the coherency and readability of the summary.

In this paper we introduce an evaluation system we have named EASY-M: **E**valuation **SY**stem for

---

[1] https://drive.google.com/file/d/1GKeJiHCAxA8fKEBpi424nmVDIHGYWKSt/view?usp=sharing

Proceedings of the Multiling 2019 Workshop, co-located with the RANLP 2019 conference, pages 53–62
Varna, Bulgaria, September 6, 2019.
http://doi.org/10.26615/978-954-452-058-8_008

Multilingiual Summarization. We have designed EASY-M for evaluation of summarization results and ranking summarization tools on multiple languages. At its current state, the system enables the user to select a language and to evaluate the quality of generic summaries using several metrics that address both informativeness and readability of summaries. EASY-M also enables users to compare the scores of evaluated summaries to corresponding scores of summaries that were produced by two baseline methods, one of which produces 'ideal' extractive summaries. By doing so, the system gives the user an idea of how far current summaries lie from the best result that can be possibly achieved by extractive summarization. EASY-M also enables the user to view the correlation between scores of different metrics with Spearman correlation.

This paper is organized as follows. Section 2 surveys related work. Section 3 describes the summarization metrics used by and the baseline summarizers implemented in EASY-M. Section 4 shows and explains system's interface. Section 5 addresses the system's availability. Finally, Section 6 concludes our work.

2 Related Work

Multiple MultiLing reports (Giannakopoulos et al., 2011, 2015, 2017) give a detailed description of evaluating multiple summarization systems in different languages for various tasks. These evaluations utilized several measures including ROUGE (Lin, 2004) and MeMoG (Giannakopoulos and Karkaletsis, 2011) for automatic evaluation of summarization systems. Both tools were applied separately and autonomously, after their adaptation to multiple languages. This experience demonstrates the actual need in the multilingual evaluation system that can be applied once on the summaries generated by different systems and rank them based on various scores measuring different summary qualities.

2.1 Automatic evaluation

Automatic evaluation relies on comparison between the summaries generated by an automatic system (*system summaries*) and summaries that have been produced by humans (called *gold standard summaries* or *reference summaries*). Reference summaries may be created from scratch by humans or produced by merging several human-produced summaries by using the majority rule (Nanba and Okumura, 2000). In both cases, reference summaries usually contain new sentences that are not present in original documents. When reference summaries are not available, system summaries may be compared to original texts through the use of a metric that helps to see how information in the whole text is covered by a summary (Jing et al., 1998). Results of automatic evaluation depend closely on the chosen metric.

2.2 Evaluation metrics

Papers (Jones and Galliers, 1995) and (Jing et al., 1998) contain surveys of early evaluation measures for text summarization. Paper (Mani, 2001) gives an overview of different methods for evaluating automatic summarization systems, and describes different evaluation criteria such as coherence, informativeness, different scoring approaches, and means of analyzing summary content.

Following (Jones and Galliers, 1995) and (Steinberger and Ježek, 2012), summarization evaluation methods can be divided into two categories: *extrinsic* evaluation, where the summary quality is judged by its helpfulness for a given task, and *intrinsic* evaluation, where a summary is analyzed directly. Our study focuses on intrinsic evaluation of generic summaries (where no user queries are supplied).

2.3 Metric types

We can roughly assign all intrinsic evaluation methods to the (1) methods comparing between system and human summaries, and (2) the methods comparing between system summaries and their documents. The metrics provided in the first category measure the closeness (similarity) of the generated summary to reference summaries that represent the ideal summaries, while the metrics calculated in the second category measure the summary's coverage of the main topics described in a document. We will call the first category "similarity" and the second one "coverage." While the "similarity" methods can be performed in either the lexical (i.e., words) or semantic (i.e., topics) level, comparison between a summary and its document in the lexical level is meaningless. Therefore, for measuring coverage of topics in a generated summary, semantic text representation must be utilized.

2.4 Lexical similarity metrics

There are multiple metrics that compare between system and reference summaries in the lexical level. These metrics measure the similarity between vocabularies (Salton and McGill, 1986) of summaries. Some of them are applicable to extractive summarization only, such as metrics based on sentence recall or precision (Kupiec et al., 1995; Jing and McKeown, 1999; Merlino and Maybury, 1999), or metrics that rely on sentence rank (in terms of summary-worthiness); they measure the correlation between sentence sequences representing system and reference summaries (Donaway et al., 2000).

The Bleu machine translation evaluation measure (Papineni et al., 2002) has been used as a summarization metric in (Pastra and Saggion, 2003).

Metrics in the Recall-Oriented Understudy for Gisting Evaluation (ROUGE) family, proposed in (Lin, 2004), count the number of overlapping units such as n-grams, word sequences, and word pairs between the system and the reference summaries. This remains the most popular metric for summarization evaluation. In (Giannakopoulos and Karkaletsis, 2011), the authors present the Merge Model Graph (MeMoG) metric for evaluating summaries, which uses n-gram graphs for comparing system and reference summaries. Tests on summaries produced for MultiLing-2015 tasks (Giannakopoulos et al., 2015) have shown a clear indication that the MeMoG is much less sensitive than ROUGE to differences in text preprocessing. Both tools are also applicable to evaluation of abstractive summaries, but, as all lexical-based methods, they do not consider semantic similarity between system and reference summaries

2.5 Semantic similarity metrics

An alternative solution to the lexical comparison between system and reference summaries is to consider their semantics. Utility-based metrics (Radev, 2000) use more fine-grained approach to measure importance of summary sentences; however, they increase the chances of disagreement between different evaluators. The Pyramid method discussed in (Nenkova and Passonneau, 2004) involves semantic matching of content units, to which differential weights are assigned based on their frequency in a corpus of summaries. Semantic models such as latent semantic analysis (LSA) (Deerwester et al.,

1990), topic modeling with latent Dirichlet analysis (LDA) (Blei et al., 2003), word embeddings with Word2Vec (Mikolov et al., 2013), and Doc2Vec (Le and Mikolov, 2014) can also be used for comparing summaries to reference summaries or to original documents. In (Steinberger and Ježek, 2012) the authors propose an LSA-based evaluation measure and show its high correlation to human rankings. In (Ng and Abrecht, 2015) and (Kusner et al., 2015) word embeddings were shown as a good means for evaluating summaries.

2.6 Readability and coherency metrics

A separate place in the world of summarization assessment metrics belongs to methods which address the linguistic quality of system-generated summaries rather than their contents. These metrics naturally depend on the language of summaries and cannot be called language-independent. We give a short description of the most popular metrics that are easy to implement with existing tools.

Proper noun ratio (PNR) is the ratio of proper nouns to the overall number of words in the summary. It is hypothesized that higher PNR indicates higher readability (Smith et al., 2012), because proper nouns contribute to a text disambiguation. Noun ratio (NR) is used to capture the proportion of nouns present in the text. The text with lower proportion of nouns is considered to be easier to read (Hancke et al., 2012). Pronoun ratio (PR) is a linguistic measure indicating the level of semantic ambiguity that can arise while searching for the concept that a pronoun represents (Štajner et al., 2012); a text with lower PR is considered more readable. The Gunning fog index (Gunning, 1952) is a readability test for English writing that gives a parametrized measurement of complex words in the text. Average word length (AWL) reflects the ratio of long words used in a text. It was proven that the use of long words makes a text more difficult to understand (Rello et al., 2013).

2.7 Evaluation systems

Attempts to create a platform for summary evaluation have been previously made. The SUMMAC system (Mani et al., 2002) provided the first system-independent framework for summary evaluation. It included several extrinsic and intrinsic methods for evaluating summaries. In the extrinsic categorization task, the evaluation was to determine whether a summary could effectively present enough information to categorize a document. In the extrinsic categorization task, an evaluation is made by finding whether there is enough information contained in a summary to provide successful categorization of the document. In an intrinsic question-answering task a topic-related summary for a document was evaluated in terms of its 'informativeness', namely, the degree to which it contained answers to a set of topic-related questions.

Paper (Hovy et al., 2006) described a framework in which various automated summary content evaluation methods can be situated, and implemented a specific variant that uses short text fragments. Multiple similarity metrics were introduced and their correlations with other known metrics, such as ROUGE, were reported. Most introduced metrics are lexical-based, except one that applied synonym resolution using WordNet. In (Abdi and Idris, 2014) the authors present a summarization assessment system that does not rely on reference summaries. There, a coverage metric was proposed as a combination of syntactic (words order) and semantic (using WordNet) information of sentence words.

Our system, EASY-M, provides different types of metric suitable for the multilingual domain and also supplies comparison to baselines, one of them being extractive topline summarizer.

3 System design

In this section we describe the capabilities of the EASY system and the algorithms it implements. The system receives the following input from the user.

1. A **folder containing original documents** in UTF-8 text format, where every document is stored in a separate file. In case of multi-document summarization, every document set should be merged into a single file.

2. A **folder containing reference summaries** should be available, with one or more summaries for every document. A document and its reference summaries are matched by their case-sensitive name parts before the file extension. Different reference summaries are distinguished by their first extension.

3. A **folder containing system summaries being evaluated**, with one summary for each document. A document and its summary are matched by a case-sensitive comparison of their name parts before file extension.

When input documents and summaries are supplied, the user first selects the language and summary size, then selects metrics (see Section 3.1) and their parameters. The pipeline of EASY-M is depicted in Figure 1. A detailed user story is described in Section 4.

3.1 Summarization quality metrics

In this section, we explain how summarization metrics are used in our system.

3.1.1 ROUGE metrics

Paper (Lin, 2004) presented set of metrics called ROUGE that is used for evaluating automatic summarization. ROUGE represents a set of similar metrics such as ROUGE-N, ROUGE-L, ROUGE-W, ROUGE-S, and ROUGE-SU. Its main idea is to count overlapping units (such as n-grams, word sequences and word pairs) between a system summary and reference summaries. Intuitively, higher ROUGE scores show that the system summary is of higher quality. This metric is currently the most popular metric of its type, especially in the field of text summarization (Cohan and Goharian, 2016).

In our system, we implemented several original ROUGE metrics and a new measure ROUGE-WSU, introduced in (Colmenares et al., 2015), as described below.

1. ROUGE-N, which measures overlap of n-grams between the system summary and reference summaries $R = \{r_1, \ldots, r_k\}$ with a user-defined n, that is usually set to a number between 1 and 4. EASY-M supports both recall- and precision-based ROUGE-N measure.

2. Common-subsequence-based metrics include the following

   (a) ROUGE-L, which measures the length of the longest common subsequence $LCS()$ between the system and reference summaries; this measure is an F-measure computed from LCS-based P_{LCS} precision and recall R_{LCS} as follows:

   $$F_{LCS} = \frac{(1 + \beta^2) R_{LCS} P_{LCS}}{R_{LCS} + \beta^2 P_{LCS}}$$

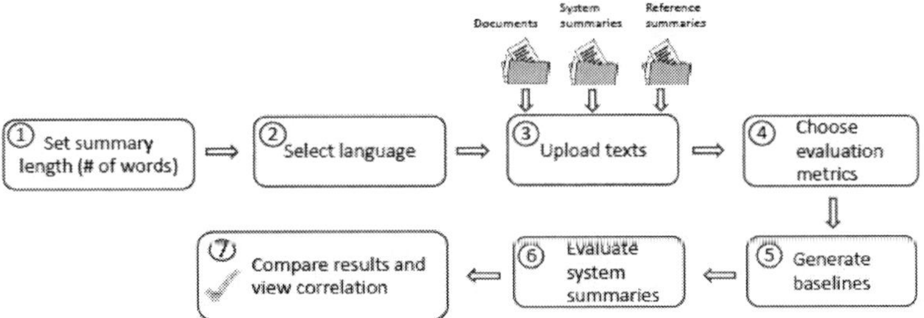

Figure 1: EASY-M system flow.

where β is the system parameter with default $\beta = 1$ (to obtain a harmonic mean).

$$P_{LCS} = \frac{\sum_{i=1}^{k} LCS(r_i, S)}{|S|}$$

$$R_{LCS} = \frac{\sum_{i=1}^{k} LCS_{\cup}(r_i, S)}{\sum_{i=1}^{k} |r_i|}$$

Here,

$$LCS_{\cup}(r_i, S) = \cup_{j=1\ldots m} LCS(r_i, s_j)$$

where $s_1, \ldots, s_m$ are the sentences of S.

(b) ROUGE-W (Lin, 2004), which measures the length of the longest weighted common subsequence and differentiates subsequences by their length. It is an F-measure F_{WLCS} of ROUGE-W precision and recall computed as:

$$R_{WLCS} = f^{-1}\left(\frac{WLCS(S, R)}{f(|S|)}\right)$$

$$P_{WLCS} = f^{-1}\left(\frac{WLCS(S, R)}{f(|r_1| + \cdots + |r_k|)}\right)$$

Function $f()$ is smooth with a smooth inverse, and is usually set to $f(k) = k^2$ so that $f^{(-1)}(k) = \sqrt{k}$. Parameter β is set to 1 (Sasaki et al., 2007).

3. Skip-based metrics

(a) ROUGE-S measures the overlap of skip-bigrams between a candidate summary and a set of reference summaries. It is similar to ROUGE-2 except that a skip-bigram refers to any pair of words in sentence order that allows for arbitrary gaps. The precision and recall are computed as a ratio of the total number of possible bigrams.

Let $SKIP2(S, r_i)$ denote the number of skip-matches between system summary S and reference summary r_i. Then ROUGE-S is defined as an F-measure R_{SKIP2} based on precision and recall on skip-bigrams where

$$R_{SKIP2} = \frac{SKIP2(S, R)}{C(|S|, 2)}$$

$$P_{SKIP2} = \frac{SKIP2(S, R)}{C(|r_1 + \cdots + r_k|, 2)}$$

and $C(x, 2)$ is the total possible number of bigrams. The maximum skip distance between two words is limited by the maximum distance parameter $d_{MAX-SKIP}$ to be 4, so that skip-bigrams are taken into account within the maximum skipping distance only.

(b) ROUGE-SU measures overlaps of both skip-bigrams and unigrams between a candidate summary and a set of reference summaries. This is because we do not want to assign a 0 score to a candidate summary simply because it does not share a skip bigram with any reference summary when instead it has a common unigram. Therefore, unigrams are added to give credit to the candidate's summary if it does not contain any pair of words with the reference summary.

(c) ROUGE-WSU weights skip-bigrams with respect to their average skip-distance. This overcomes the main problem of ROUGE-SU that gives the same importance to all skip-bigrams extracted from a phrase.

3.1.2 MeMoG metric

The MeMoG metric, presented in (Giannakopoulos and Karkaletsis, 2011), is an evaluation method that based on n-gram graphs. Experimental proof of its high performance for evaluation of summaries in different languages is presented in (Giannakopoulos et al., 2015).

Given a set of reference summaries, the MeMoG metric creates an n-gram graph for each of them and an n-gram graph for the system summary. Formally, let $G = \{V, E, W\}$ be an n-gram graph, where V is the set of character n-grams that can be created from the text, E is the set of edges, and W is the weight function that represents the number of times a pair of n-grams is present in a text within a legal distance from each other. This distance is denoted D_{win}. In order to compute this metric, the user should supply the following parameters:

1. L_{min} - minimum length of n-grams,

2. L_{max} - maximum length of n-grams, and

3. D_{win} - the windows size for two n-grams.

The default parameters are $L_{min} = 3$, $L_{max} = 3$ and $D_{win} = 3$, following (Giannakopoulos and Karkaletsis, 2011). The next step is to represent all reference summaries by a single n-gram graph. We begin by initializing the graph to be an n-gram graph of any of the reference summaries. The initial graph is then updated using every one of the remaining n-gram reference summary graphs as follows. Let G_1 be the current merged n-gram graph, and let G_2 be the n-gram graph of the next reference summary. The *merge function* $U(G_1, G_2, l)$ defined edge weights as

$$w(e) = w^1(e) + (w^2(e) - w^1(e)) * l$$

where $l \in [0, 1]$ is the learning factor, $w^1(e)$ is the weight of e in G_1, and $w^2(e)$ is the weight of e in G_2. In our system we chose $l = \frac{1}{i}$ where $i > 1$ is the number of the reference graph being processed. In the MeMoG metric, the score of a summary is one similarity measurement, denoted by VS, between system summary graph G^j

and the merged reference graph G^i. The similarity score between edges is defined as

$$VR(e) = \min\{w^i(e), w^j(e)\}/\max\{w^i(e), w^j(e)\}$$

where w^i and w^j are weights of the same edge e (identified by its end-node labels) in graphs G^i and G^j respectively. The final score is computed as

$$VS(G^i, G^j) = \sum VR(e)/\max\{|G^i|, |G^j|\}$$

3.2 Topic coverage metrics

Topic model is a type of statistical model for discovering the abstract topics that occur in a collection of documents. Latent Dirichlet allocation (LDA) (Blei et al., 2003; Blei, 2012) allows documents to have a mixture of topics. LDA uses a generative probabilistic approach for discovering the abstract topics, (i.e., clusters of semantically coherent documents). As a result, we assume that every word w in document D is assigned its probability distribution $\{p_{w,T_i}\}$ over topics $T_1, \ldots, T_K$ where K is the number of topics supplied as a user-defined parameter. Then for a system summary S we can naturally define topic similarity to document (TSD) and topic similarity to reference summary (TSR) metrics as follows:

1. For every word w, its topic $T(w)$ is set to be $T(w) = \arg\max_i p_{w,T_i}$.

2. A text is represented by topic vector $TV = (p_{w,T_i})_w$ of word topics; if word w is not present in the text, $TV[w] = 0$.

3. Topic similarity between document D and system summary S is computed as cosine similarity $TSD(D, S) = \cos(TV_S, TV_D)$ between their topic vectors.

4. Topic similarity between system summary S and reference summaries $r_1, \ldots, r_n$ is computed as maximal cosine similarity between their topic vectors: $TSR(r_1, \ldots, r_n, S) = \max_i \cos(TV_S, TV_{r_i})$

3.3 Readability metrics

In our system we implemented proper noun ratio (PNR), noun ratio (NR), pronoun ratio (PR), and average word length (AWL) metrics. Currently, these metrics are supported for the English language only.

3.4 Baselines

3.4.1 TopK baseline

For this baseline, we simply select the first K sentences of the source document so that the number of words of the candidate summary is at least the predefined word limit W, making K minimal.

3.4.2 OCCAMS baseline

The OCCAMS, introduced in (Davis et al., 2012), is an algorithm for selecting sentences from a source document when reference summaries are known. This algorithm finds the best possible sentence subset covering reference summaries because reference summaries are visible to it. While no extractive summary can fully match human-generated abstractive reference summaries, OC-CAMS achieves the best possible result (or its good approximation) for the extractive summarization task. Comparing system summaries to the result of OCCAMS shows exactly how far the tested system is from realistic best possible extractive summarization result.

The OCCAMS' parameters are the weights of the terms W, the number of words in sentences C, and the size of the candidate summary L. Let D be the source document consisting of sentences $S_1, \ldots, S_n$ and let $T = \{t_1, \ldots, t_m\}$ be the set of document's terms (tokenized stemmed words). Initially OCCAMS computes document matrix A using term-to-sentence assignment and term entropy weights. Then, OCCAMS computes the singular value decomposition of matrix A as $A = USV^T$, following the approach of (Steinberger and Ježek, 2004). The singular value decomposition produces term weights $w(t_i)$. Then, the final solution is computed by using Budgeted Maximum Coverage (BMC) from (Khuller et al., 1999) and Fully Polynomial Time Approximation Scheme (FPTAS) of (Karger, 2001) greedy algorithms. These algorithms select sentences that provide maximum coverage of the important terms (maximum weight sum), while ensuring that their total length does not exceed the intended summary size.

4 Implementation details

In this section we describe and give examples of the EASY system interface. [2]

---

[2]Screen images are taken from standalone implementation. Web implementation with partial features

4.1 Operational pipeline

The first screen of the system (see Figure 2) asks the user to choose language and to set the summary length (if a summary is too long, it will be cut to the given number of words).

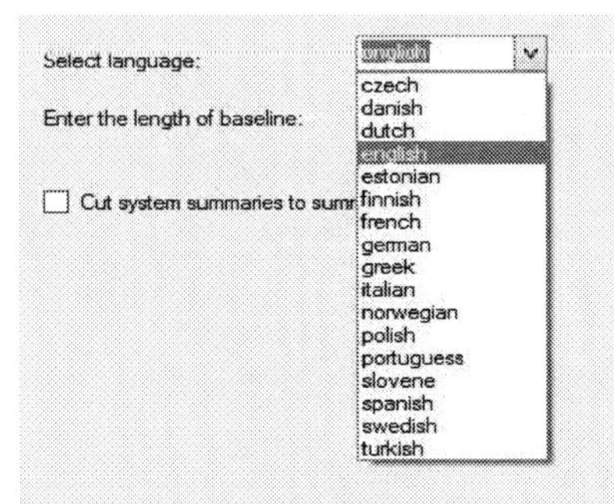

Figure 2: Choosing language.

In our system, a user can make a choice between analyzing a single file with its system and reference summaries, or analyzing an entire corpus. The user needs to supply file names for the document (or directory of documents), reference summary (or summaries) or reference summaries directory, and the system summary or their directory that is to be evaluated. File names are treated as case-sensitive. Figure 3 shows the input selection interface for the case of a corpus.

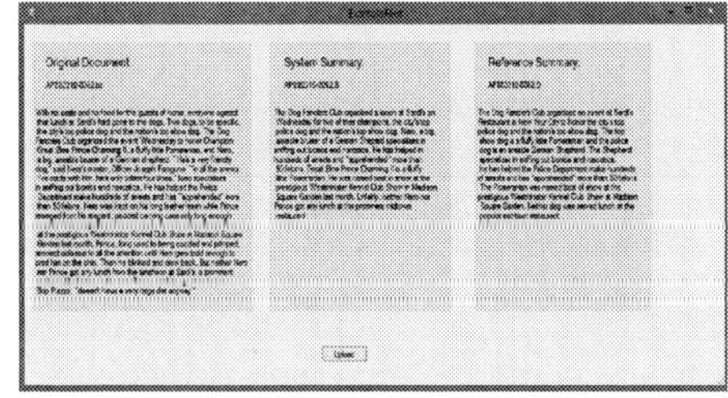

Figure 3: Choosing texts, reference and system summary.

Figures 4, 5 and 6 show results of computation for ROUGE, MeMoG, and topic summarization metrics and readability metrics for the selected input. Note that readability analysis is currently supported for the English language only. The top part of the interface in both cases enables the user to select parameters for every metric, while the bottom

---

is also available at https://summaryevaluation.azurewebsites.net/home.

part gives the user an opportunity to compute baseline summaries and to compute the chosen metric for baselines with the same parameters as above.

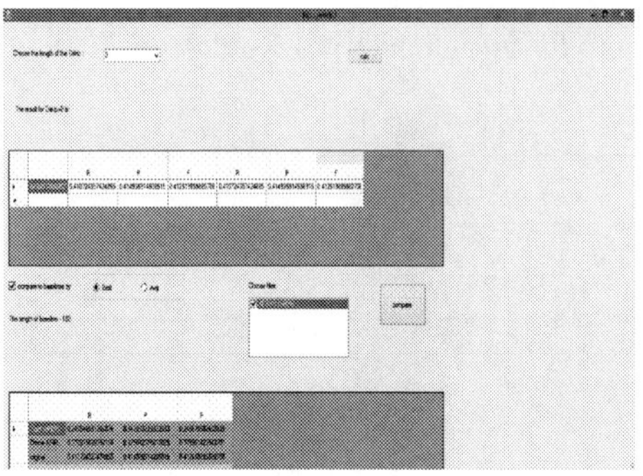

Figure 4: Rouge metrics computation with comparison to baselines.

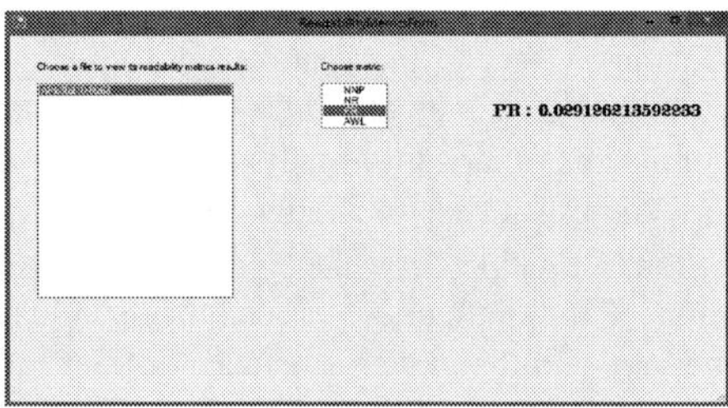

Figure 5: Readability metrics computation.

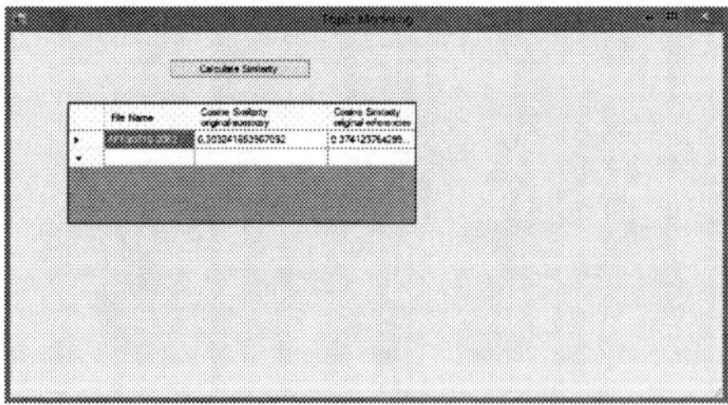

Figure 6: Topic metrics computation.

Figure 7 shows baseline summary computed by the OCCAMS algorithm.

5   Availability and reproducibility

The EASY-M system standalone version is implemented in c#, and its Web version is implemented in Angular7 on the client side, and sp.net WebAPI2 on the server side. Video of the standalone interface operation is available at `https://www.youtube.com/watch?v=HQhzhSQ7O1A&t=143s`. Currently, the system

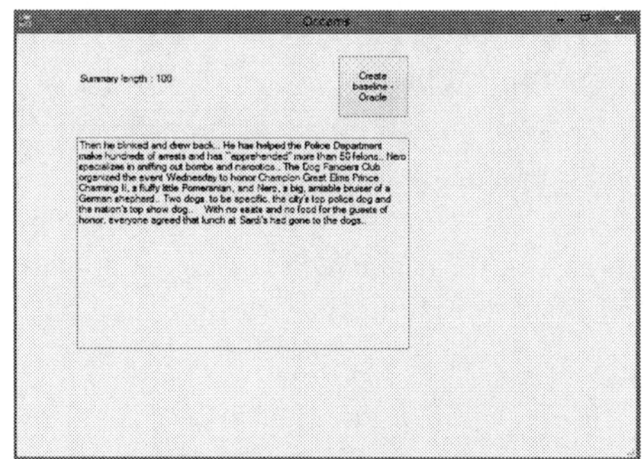

Figure 7: OCCAMS summary.

supports 17 languages: Czech, Danish, Dutch, English, Estonian, Finnish, French, German, Greek, Italian, Norwegian, Polish, Portuguese, Slovene, Spanish, Swedish and Turkish.

6   Conclusions

In this paper we present a multilingual framework named EASY-M for evaluation of automatic summarization systems. Currently, EASY-M supports 17 different languages. The system enables the users to compute several summarization metrics, including readability measures (English only), for the same set of summaries and to observe how they correlate with each other using Spearsman's correlation.

In our future work we plan to implement additional metrics based on word embeddings, and to add more languages by employing language specific tokenizer tools. We also plan to implement additional baseline methods. We will allow several systems to be compared and ranked simultaneously.

References

Asad Abdi and Norisma Idris. 2014. Automated summarization assessment system: quality assessment without a reference summary. In *The International Conference on Advances in Applied Science and Environmental Engineering-ASEE*.

D M Blei. 2012. Probabilistic topic models. *Communications of the ACM* 55(4):77–84.

D. M. Blei, A. Y. Ng, and M. I. Jordan. 2003. Latent dirichlet allocation. *Journal of Machine Learning Research* 3:993–1022.

Arman Cohan and Nazli Goharian. 2016. Revisiting summarization evaluation for scientific articles. *arXiv preprint arXiv:1604.00400* .

Carlos A Colmenares, Marina Litvak, Amin Mantrach, and Fabrizio Silvestri. 2015. Heads: Headline generation as sequence prediction using an abstract feature-rich space. In *Proceedings of the 2015 Conference of the North American Chapter of the Association for Computational Linguistics: Human Language Technologies*. pages 133–142.

Dipanjan Das and André FT Martins. 2007. A survey on automatic text summarization. *Literature Survey for the Language and Statistics II course at CMU* 4:192–195.

Sashka T Davis, John M Conroy, and Judith D Schlesinger. 2012. OCCAMS–an optimal combinatorial covering algorithm for multi-document summarization. In *Data Mining Workshops (ICDMW), 2012 IEEE 12th International Conference on*. IEEE, pages 454–463.

Scott Deerwester, Susan T Dumais, George W Furnas, Thomas K Landauer, and Richard Harshman. 1990. Indexing by latent semantic analysis. *Journal of the American society for information science* 41(6):391–407.

Robert L Donaway, Kevin W Drummey, and Laura A Mather. 2000. A comparison of rankings produced by summarization evaluation measures. In *Proceedings of the 2000 NAACL-ANLP Workshop on Automatic summarization*. Association for Computational Linguistics, pages 69–78.

Mahak Gambhir and Vishal Gupta. 2017. Recent automatic text summarization techniques: a survey. *Artificial Intelligence Review* 47(1):1–66

George Giannakopoulos, John Conroy, Jeff Kubina, Peter A Rankel, Elena Lloret, Josef Steinberger, Marina Litvak, and Benoit Favre. 2017. Multiling 2017 overview. In *Proceedings of the MultiLing 2017 workshop on summarization and summary evaluation across source types and genres*. pages 1–6.

George Giannakopoulos, Mahmoud El-Haj, Benoit Favre, Marina Litvak, Josef Steinberger, and Vasudeva Varma. 2011. TAC 2011 MultiLing pilot overview. In *Proceedings of Text Analytics Conference*. TAC.

George Giannakopoulos and Vangelis Karkaletsis. 2011. AutoSummENG and MeMoG in evaluating guided summaries. In *Proceedings of Text Analysis Conference*.

George Giannakopoulos, Jeff Kubina, John Conroy, Josef Steinberger, Benoit Favre, Mijail Kabadjov, Udo Kruschwitz, and Massimo Poesio. 2015. Multiling 2015: multilingual summarization of single and multi-documents, on-line fora, and call-center conversations. In *Proceedings of the 16th Annual Meeting of the Special Interest Group on Discourse and Dialogue*. pages 270–274.

Robert Gunning. 1952. *The technique of clear writing*. McGraw-Hill, New York.

Vishal Gupta and Gurpreet Singh Lehal. 2010. A survey of text summarization extractive techniques. *Journal of emerging technologies in web intelligence* 2(3):258–268.

Julia Hancke, Sowmya Vajjala, and Detmar Meurers. 2012. Readability classification for german using lexical, syntactic, and morphological features. *Proceedings of COLING 2012* pages 1063–1080.

Eduard Hovy, Chin-Yew Lin, Liang Zhou, and Junichi Fukumoto. 2006. Automated summarization evaluation with basic elements. In *Proceedings of the Fifth Conference on Language Resources and Evaluation (LREC 2006)*. Citeseer, pages 604–611.

Hongyan Jing, Regina Barzilay, Kathleen McKeown, and Michael Elhadad. 1998. Summarization evaluation methods: Experiments and analysis. In *AAAI symposium on intelligent summarization*. Palo Alto, CA, pages 51–59.

Hongyan Jing and Kathleen R McKeown. 1999. The decomposition of human-written summary sentences. In *Proceedings of the 22nd annual international ACM SIGIR conference on Research and development in information retrieval*. ACM, pages 129–136.

Karen Sparck Jones and Julia R Galliers. 1995. *Evaluating natural language processing systems: An analysis and review*, volume 1083. Springer Science & Business Media.

David R Karger. 2001. A randomized fully polynomial time approximation scheme for the all-terminal network reliability problem. *SIAM review* 43(3):499–522.

NR Kasture, Neha Yargal, Neha Nityanand Singh, Neha Kulkarni, and Vijay Mathur. 2014. A survey on methods of abstractive text summarization. *Int. J. Res. Merg. Sci. Technol* 1(6):53–57.

Samir Khuller, Anna Moss, and Joseph Seffi Naor. 1999. The budgeted maximum coverage problem. *Information processing letters* 70(1):39–45.

Julian Kupiec, Jan Pedersen, and Francine Chen. 1995. A trainable document summarizer. In *Proceedings of the 18th annual international ACM SIGIR conference on Research and development in information retrieval*. ACM, pages 68–73.

Matt Kusner, Yu Sun, Nicholas Kolkin, and Kilian Weinberger. 2015. From word embeddings to document distances. In *International Conference on Machine Learning*. pages 957–966.

Quoc Le and Tomas Mikolov. 2014. Distributed representations of sentences and documents. In *International Conference on Machine Learning*. pages 1188–1196.

Chin-Yew Lin. 2004. ROUGE: A package for automatic evaluation of summaries. In *Proceedings of the Workshop on Text Summarization Branches Out (WAS 2004)*. pages 25–26.

Elena Lloret and Manuel Palomar. 2012. Text summarisation in progress: a literature review. *Artificial Intelligence Review* 37(1):1–41.

Inderjeet Mani. 2001. Summarization evaluation: An overview. In *NAACL 2001 Workshop on Automatic Summarization*.

Inderjeet Mani, Gary Klein, David House, Lynette Hirschman, Therese Firmin, and Beth Sundheim. 2002. SUMMAC: a text summarization evaluation. *Natural Language Engineering* 8(1):43–68.

Andrew Merlino and Mark Maybury. 1999. *An empirical study of the optimal presentation of multimedia summaries of broadcast news*. Cambridge, MA: MIT Press.

Tomas Mikolov, Ilya Sutskever, Kai Chen, Greg S Corrado, and Jeff Dean. 2013. Distributed representations of words and phrases and their compositionality. In *Advances in neural information processing systems*. pages 3111–3119.

Hidetsugu Nanba and Manabu Okumura. 2000. Producing more readable extracts by revising them. In *Proceedings of the 18th conference on Computational linguistics-Volume 2*. pages 1071–1075.

Ani Nenkova and Kathleen McKeown. 2012. A survey of text summarization techniques. In *Mining text data*, Springer, pages 43–76.

Ani Nenkova, Kathleen McKeown, et al. 2011. Automatic summarization. *Foundations and Trends in Information Retrieval* 5(2–3):103–233.

Ani Nenkova and Rebecca Passonneau. 2004. Evaluating content selection in summarization: The pyramid method. In *Proceedings of the human language technology conference of the north american chapter of the association for computational linguistics: Hlt-naacl 2004*.

Jun-Ping Ng and Viktoria Abrecht. 2015. Better summarization evaluation with word embeddings for rouge. *arXiv preprint arXiv:1508.06034* .

Kishore Papineni, Salim Roukos, Todd Ward, and Wei-Jing Zhu. 2002. Bleu: a method for automatic evaluation of machine translation. In *Proceedings of the 40th annual meeting on association for computational linguistics*. Association for Computational Linguistics, pages 311–318.

Katerina Pastra and Horacio Saggion. 2003. Colouring summaries bleu. In *Proceedings of the EACL 2003 Workshop on Evaluation Initiatives in Natural Language Processing: are evaluation methods, metrics and resources reusable?*. Association for Computational Linguistics, pages 35–42.

Nikiforos Pittaras, Stefano Montanelliy, George Giannakopoulos, Alfio Ferraray, and Vangelis Karkaletsis. 2019. Crowdsourcing in single-document summary evaluation: the argo way. In Marina Litvak and Natalia Vanetik, editors, *Multilingual Text Analysis: Challenges, Models, and Approaches*, World Scientific, chapter 8.

Dragomir R Radev. 2000. Summarization of multiple documents: clustering, sentence extraction, and evaluation. In *Proceedings of the Workshop on Automatic Summarization, 2000*. Association for Computational Linguistics.

Luz Rello, Ricardo Baeza-Yates, Laura Dempere-Marco, and Horacio Saggion. 2013. Frequent words improve readability and short words improve understandability for people with dyslexia. In *IFIP Conference on Human-Computer Interaction*. Springer, pages 203–219.

Gerard Salton and Michael J McGill. 1986. *Introduction to modern information retrieval*. McGraw-Hill, Inc.

Yutaka Sasaki et al. 2007. The truth of the F-measure. *Teach Tutor mater* 1(5):1–5.

Christian Smith, Henrik Danielsson, and Arne Jönsson. 2012. A good space: Lexical predictors in vector space evaluation. In *Proceedings of the eighth international conference on Language Resources and Evaluation (LREC), Istanbul, Turkey*. Citeseer.

Sanja Štajner, Richard Evans, Constantin Orasan, and Ruslan Mitkov. 2012. What can readability measures really tell us about text complexity. In *Proceedings of workshop on natural language processing for improving textual accessibility*. Citeseer, pages 14–22.

Josef Steinberger and Karel Ježek. 2004. Text summarization and singular value decomposition. In *International Conference on Advances in Information Systems*. Springer, pages 245–254.

Josef Steinberger and Karel Ježek. 2012. Evaluation measures for text summarization. *Computing and Informatics* 28(2):251–275.

A study of semantic augmentation of word embeddings for extractive summarization

Nikiforos Pittaras
DIT, NKUA
IIT, NCSR-D
npittaras@di.uoa.gr

Vangelis Karkaletsis
IIT, NCSR-D
vangelis@iit.demokritos.gr

Abstract

In this study we examine the effect of semantic augmentation approaches on extractive text summarization. Wordnet hypernym relations are used to extract term-frequency concept information, subsequently concatenated to sentence level representations produced by aggregated deep neural word embeddings. Multiple dimensionality reduction techniques and combination strategies are examined via feature transformation and clustering methods. An experimental evaluation on the MultiLing 2015 MSS dataset illustrates that semantic information can introduce benefits to the extractive summarization process in terms of F1, ROUGE-1 and ROUGE-2 scores, with LSA-based postprocessing introducing the largest improvements.

1 Introduction

In recent years, the abundance of textual information resulting from the proliferation of the Internet, online journalism and personal blogging platforms has led to the need for automatic summarization tools. These solutions can aid users to navigate the saturated information marketplace efficiently via the production of digestible summaries that retain the core content of the original text (Yogan et al., 2016). At the same time, advancements introduced by deep learning techniques have provided efficient representation methods for text, mainly via the development of dense, low-dimensional vector representations for words and sentences (LeCun et al., 2015). Additionally, semantic information sources have been compiled by humans in a structured manner and are available for use towards aiding a variety of natural language process-

ing applications. As a result, semantic augmentation approaches can introduce existing knowledge to the neural pipeline, circumventing the need for the neural model to learn all useful information from scratch.

In this study, we examine the effect of semantic augmentation and post-processing techniques on extractive summarization performance. Specifically, we modify the input features of a deep neural classification model by injecting semantic features, simultaneously employing feature transformation post-processing methods towards dimensionality reduction and discrimination optimization. Specifically, we aim to address the following research questions.

- Can the introduction of semantic information in the network input improve extractive summarization performance?

- Does the semantic augmentation process benefit via dimensionality reduction postprocessing methods?

The rest of the paper is structure as follows. In section 2 we cover existing related work relevant to this study. This is followed by a description of our approach (section 3). In section 4 we outline our experimental methodology and discuss on results and findings. Finally, we present our conclusions in section 5.

2 Related work

2.1 Text representations

Extensive research has investigated methods of representing text for Natural Language Processing and Machine Learning tasks.

Vector Space Model (VSM) approaches project the input to a n-dimensional vector representation, exploiting properties of vector spaces and lin-

Proceedings of the Multiling 2019 Workshop, co-located with the RANLP 2019 conference, pages 63–72
Varna, Bulgaria, September 6, 2019.
http://doi.org/10.26615/978-954-452-058-8_009

ear algebra techniques for cross-document operations. Approaches like the Bag-of-Words (Salton et al., 1975) have become popular baselines, mapping the occurence of an input term (e.g. a word) to their occurence frequencies in the text. Modifications to the model include refinements in the term weighting strategy such as DF and TF-IDF normalizations (Yang, 1997; Salton and Buckley, 1988), term preprocessing such as stemming and lemmatization (Jivani et al., 2011), and others. Further, sentence and phrase-level terms are examined (Scott and Matwin, 1999), along with n-gram approaches, which consider n-tuple occurences of terms instead (Brown et al., 1992; Katz, 2003; Post and Bergsma, 2013).

Other approaches encode term co-occurence information via representation learning, relying on the distributional hypothesis (Harris, 1954) to capture semantic content. At the same time, the need to circumvent the curse of dimensionality (Hastie et al., 2005) of term-weight feature vectors has led to the production dense, rather than sparse representations. Early such examples used analytic matrix decompositions on co-occurence statistics (Jolliffe, 2011; Deerwester et al., 1990; Horn and Johnson, 2012), while more recently, vector embeddings are iteratively optimized learned by analyzing large text corpora using local word context in a sliding window fashion (Mikolov et al., 2013a,b), or using pre-computed pairwise word co-occurences (Pennington et al., 2014). More refined methods break down words to subword units (Bojanowski et al., 2017), where learning representations for the latter enables some success in handling out-of-vocabulary words.

2.2 Extractive summarization

In summarization, contrary to the abstractive approach where output summaries are generated from scratch (Yogan et al., 2016), the extractive method relies on sentence salience detection to retain a minimal subset of the most informative sentences in the original text (Gupta and Lehal, 2010). VSM approaches have been widely utilized in sentence modelling for this task, with a variety of methods for determining term weights based on word frequency, probability, mutual information or tf-idf features, sentence similarity, as well as a variety of feature combination methods (Mori, 2002; McCargar, 2004; Nenkova and Vanderwende, 2005; Galley et al., 2006; Lloret and Palomar, 2009). Other popular handcrafted features used are syntactic / grammar information such as part-of-speech tags, as well as sentencewise features such as sentence position and length. Finally, similarity scores to title, centroid clusters and predefined keywords can be used to score / rank sentences towards salience identification and extraction (Neto et al., 2002; Yogan et al., 2016).

Other works adopt a topic-based approach, using topic modelling techniques towards sentence salience detection. For example, the work in (Aries et al., 2015) builds topics via a clustering process, using a word and sentence-level vector space model and the cosine similarity measure. Clustering techniques have been applied to this end, for sentence grouping and subsequent salience identification (Radev et al., 2000).

Graph methods have also been exploited; In (Lawrie et al., 2001), the authors adopt a graph-based probabilistic language model towards building a topic hierarchy for predicting representative vocabulary terms. The MUSE system (Litvak and Last, 2013) combines graph-modelling with genetic algorithms towards sentence modelling and subsequent ranking, while the work in (Mihalcea and Tarau, 2004) builds sentence graphs using a variety of feature bags and similarity measures and proceeds to extract central sentences via multiple iterations of the TextRank algorithm.

2.3 Semantic enrichment

Semantic information has been broadly exploited towards aiding NLP tasks, using resources such as Wordnet (Miller, 1995), Freebase (Bollacker et al., 2008), Framenet (Baker et al., 1998) and others. Such external knowledge bases have seen widespread use, ranging from early works on expanson of rule-based discrimination techniques (Scott and Matwin, 1998), to synonym-based feature extraction (Rodriguez et al., 2000) and large-scale feature generation from WordNet synset relationships edges for SVM classification (Mansuy and Hilderman, 2006).

In extractive summarization, semantic information has been used as a refinement step in the sentence salience detection pipeline. For example, in (Dang and Luo, 2008), the authors utilize WordNet synsets as a keyphrase ranking mechanism, based on candidate synset relevance to the text. Other approaches (Vicente et al., 2015) use semantic features from Wordnet and named entity extraction, followed by a PCA-based post-processing step for dimensionality reduction. Wordnet is also utilized in (Li et al., 2017) where the authors use the resource for sentence similarity extraction, using synset similarity on the word level and treating the resulting scores as additional features for summarization and citation linkage.

Our approach bears some similarities with the work of (Vicente et al., 2015), extending the investigation to additional post-processing techniques to PCA, examining post-processing application strategies, and adopting deep neural word embeddings as the lexical representation, while grounding on a number of baselines. In the following section, we will describe our approach in detail, including text representation, semantic feature extraction, training and evaluation.

3 Proposed Method

3.1 Problem definition

We formulate the task of automatic summarization as a classification problem. Given a document consisting of N sentences $D = \{s_1, s_2, \ldots s_N\}$ and a ground truth (extractive) summary of size k, $G = \{g_1, g_2, \ldots g_k\}$, $g_i \in D$, a classification-based extractive summarization system F selects salient sentences $P = \{p_1, p_2, \ldots p_k\}$ via $F(D) = P$, such that P is as close to G as possible. In this work, $F(\cdot)$ is a data-driven machine learning model, built by exploiting statistical features in the input text.

3.2 Text representation

We use a variety of approaches for representing the textual component of a sentence. First, we employ Continuous Bag-of-Words (CBOW) variant of the popular word2vec model (Mikolov et al., 2013b), which builds vector representations of a word using a statistical language model that predicts the word based on its surrounding context. More formally, given a center word in a sentence, w_c and and a set of $2k$ context words around it $w_{context} = [w_{c-k} \ldots, w_{c-1}, w_{c+1}, \ldots, w_{c+k}]$, CBOW tries to optimize the conditional probabilistic neural language model $P(w_c|w_{context})$.

We train embeddings from scratch with this method, optimizing with the cross-entropy loss, ending up with a vector representation for each word in the dataset. We subsequently produce the final, sentence-level representation by averaging the vectors corresponding to words in a sentence.

In addition to embedding training, we examine the performance of pre-trained Fastext (Joulin et al., 2016) embeddings, produced by a model that captures subword information via character embeddings, enabling handling of out-of-vocabulary words. Additionally, we employ direct sentence-level modelling alternatives via the doc2vec (Le and Mikolov, 2014) extension of word2vec, as well as a sentence-level TF-IDF baseline.

3.3 Semantic representation

In order to capture and utilize semantic information in the text, we use the WordNet semantic graph (Miller, 1995), a lexical database for English, often used as an external information source for machine learning research in classification, summarization, clustering and other tasks (Hung and Wermter, 2004; Elberrichi et al., 2008; Liu et al., 2007; Morin and Bengio, 2005; Bellare et al., 2004; Dang and Luo, 2008; Pal and Saha, 2014). In Wordnet, semantic relations between concepts are captured in a semantic graph of synonymous sets (*synsets*), as well as multiple types of relations of lexical / semantic nature, such as ike hypernymy and hyponymy (is-a graph edges), meronymy (part-of relations, and others). We employ WordNet as an enrichment mechanism, extracting frequency-based features from corpus words. Specifically, we mine semantic concepts from each word in the text, arriving at a sparse high-dimensional bag-of-concepts for each document. This vector is concatenated to the lexical representation. To deal with the curse of dimensionality (Hastie et al., 2005) of this approach, we apply dimensionality reduction via PCA (Jolliffe, 2011), LSA (Deerwester et al., 1990) or K-Means (Lloyd, 1982). We apply each transformation on two settings; first, the semantic information channel is reduced, then concatenated with the sentence embedding vector. Alternatively, we apply the reduction on the concatenated, enriched vector itself.

4 Experiments

4.1 Datasets

We use the english version of the Multiling 2015 single-document summarization dataset (Giannakopoulos et al., 2015; Conroy et al., 2015) [1] for our experimental evaluation. The dataset is

[1] http://multiling.iit.demokritos.gr/
pages/view/1516/multiling-2015

feature	train	test
document sentences	233	184.9
document summary sentences	77.9	13.5
document words	25.5	22.8
samples	6990	5546

Table 1: Details of the Multiling 2015 single-document summarization dataset. All values are averages accross documents, except from the number of samples.

built from wikipedia content, consisting of articles paired with a number of human-authored summaries. For each of 40 languages, 30 documents and summary sets are provided.

In this work, we focus on the English version of the dataset, due to our reliance on word embedding features, which are predomninantly available for the English language. In addition, we apply two preprocessing steps. First, we reformat the ground truth towards an extractive summarization setting, since the provided summaries are written from scratch. Specifically, we annotate source sentences with an extractive summarization binary label $l \in \{0,1\}$ (e.g. 1 if it is a member of the extractive summary and 0 otherwise). This is accomplised via the following steps. First, for each provided summary sentence p_i, we rank source sentences $s \in S$ with respect to the n-gram overlap with p_i, after stopword filtering and excluding already positively-labelled sentences $s_j \in S : l_j = 1, i \neq j$. The top-ranked source sentence is matched to the ground truth summary sentence, and considered to be a member of the extractive summary. Secondly, in an effort to address the severe imbalance that results from the modifications of previous step (i.e. class 0 being 13 to 14 times more populous than class 1), we oversample positively labelled sentences for each document, arriving at a $2 : 1$ negative to positive ratio, at most.

After these steps, we end up with the final version of the dataset which is described in detail in table 1. Having a sentence-level label for summary meronymy, we can thus produce the final summary by concatenating the positively classified sentences. It should be noted that via this setting, evaluating candidate summaries with the dataset provided ground truth summaries implies a minimum performance penalty. This is reported in the results in the succeeding section 4.3.

4.2 Setup

We train embeddings with the word2vec CBOW variant using gensim (Rehurek and Sojka, 2011). We run the algorithm for 50 epochs, on a 10-word window, mantaining a minimum word frequency threshold of 2 occurences in the training text. We produce 50-dimensional embeddings via this process. In addition, we use the publicly available [2], 300-dimensional pre-trained fastext embeddings for the corresponding configuration.

To setup the deep neural classifier, we run a grid search on the number of layers (ranging from 1 to 5) and layer size (ranging from 64 to 2048) for a multilayer perceptron architecture, using a 5-fold validation scheme. This process illustrated a 5-layer architecture of 512-neuron layers as the best performing, and is the one we adopt for all subsequent experiments. This architecture is trained for 80 epochs, reducing the learning rate on an adaptive learning rate reduction policy and mantaining an early-stopping protocol of 25 epochs.

Using this learning framework, we test each candidate configuration using a 5-fold validated scheme, reporting mean measure values as the overall result. For all measures, the cross-fold variance stayed below $10e - 4$ and is omitted. The Keras machine learning library [3] is used for building and training the neural models.

4.3 Results and discussion

Tables 2 and 3 present experimental results for the evaluation of semantic augmentation on word2vec and fastext embeddings, respectively. Each configuration is evaluated in terms of micro and macro F1 score (`mi-F` and `ma-F` columns, respectively), with respect to classification performance of the oversampled dataset (as detailed in 4.1). In addition, we measure Rouge-1 and Rouge-2 scores of the final composed summary (stiched together from positively classified input sentences) with respect to the hand-written ground truth summary provided in the dataset. Since the difference between the latter two guarantees a minimum error (see 4.1), we report the best possible performance in the `gt` configuration, depicting performance for each evaluation measure when sentence classification is perfect. In addition, via the `prob` configuration we report a probabilistic baseline classifier, which decides based on the label distribution

---

[2]https://fasttext.cc/
[3]https://keras.io/

in the training data. Moreover, token frequency-based baselines – namely bag-of-words (BOW) and TF-IDF (Salton and Buckley, 1988) – are reported in the `BOW` and `TF-IDF` rows. Lexical-only and semantically-augmented baseline runs are reported as `x` and `x-sem` respectively, where $x \in [w2v, fastext]$. Finally, the effect of each post-processing method on the semantically augmented baseline is illustrated, where a configuration of `+conf-N` denotes a vector post-processing method `conf` that produces `N`-dimensional vectors. The resulting vector dimension that is fed to the classfier is reported in the column `dim`, and the different semantic augmentation post-processing methods are denoted by `tc` – i.e. first transform the semantic channel, then concatenate to the embedding – and `ct` – i.e. concatenate the semantic vector to the lexical embedding, then apply the transformation.

Regarding word2vec trained embedings (table 2), we can see that introducing semantic information improves macro F1, Rouge-1, Rouge-2 performance. Compared with the bag-based baselines, we observe the word2vec CBOW embeddings yielding worse micro F1 performance than both bag approaches, but considerably better Rouge scores. In addition, the semantically enriched `w2v` configuration outperforms the bag approaches in macro-F1 score and the examined Rouge measures.

In general, we observe that micro-F1 scores appear to be less reliable measures in this setting, given the considerable large class imbalance of the dataset. This is apparent in the baseline `w2v` and `w2v-sem` baseline runs, however the effect is most pronounced in k-means configurations for dimensions greater than 50, where the best micro-F1 score is encountered, but the performance of all other metrics is degenerate. This is understandable, since cases where the classifier completely relies on the majority class (0, or "non-summary sentences" in our case), it can converge to a state characterized by a total lack of positively classified sentences. This in turn produces zero rouge scores and sub-chance macro-averaged F1 scores, which is the case observed for these configurations. The best-performing configuration turns out to be LSA with 500-dimensional vectors, with regard to Rouge-1 and Rouge-2 scores, with the 100-dimensional PCA configuration performing best in terms of macro F1.

Regarding comparison between the two post-processing strategies, we can observe that `tc` appears to be working slightly better when measuring micro-F1 scores, but in terms of macro-F1 and Rouge scores, concatenating prior to post-processing works considerably better. This is not surprising, as the transformation of the bimodal vector into a common, shared space can be expected to be a far more efficient fusion of the lexical and semantic channels, compared to simple concatenation.

Regarding fastext-based runs, a similar baseline performance is observed. Bag-based baselines achieve best micro-F1 score, but inferior results in all other measures. Similarly to word2vec, the lexical-only fastext run achieves better F1 scores, however the semantically enriched embedding fares far better in terms of Rouge-1 and Rouge-2 performance. Likewise, similar behavior is observed with regard to post-processing and concatenation order and the usefulness of the micro-F1 score compared to the other measures. Notably, the 50-dimensional LSA performs well with the `tc` strategy, while an analogous degenerate behaviour is evident with the K-means configurations. As in the word2vec run, the 500-dimensional LSA produces the best macro-F1 and Rouge scores.

Comparing the word2vec and fastext-based runs, we can observe the word2vec configurations (trained on the target dataset from scratch) achieve better Rouge-1 and Rouge-2 scores than the pre-trained fastext embeddings, on the best configurations of both baseline and best performing post-processed configurations (500 dimensional LSA).

In light of these results, we return to the research questions stated in the beginning of this document.

- **Can the introduction of semantic information in the network input improve extractive summarization performance?**

  It appears that the introduction of semantic information can introduce benefits to the extractive summarization pipeline. This is illustrated by the Rouge scores, which are considerably improved in the augmented configurations, for both embeddings examined. On the contrary, micro / macro-F1 results are either not significantly affected or can even deteriorate. However, as discussed above, we argue that the severe class imbalance of the dataset

config	dim	mi-F		ma-F		Rouge-1		Rouge-2	
gt	N/A	1.000		1.000		0.414		0.132	
prob	N/A	0.871		0.501		0.051		0.009	
BOW	15852	0.9254		0.5131		0.094		0.017	
TF-IDF	15852	0.9260		0.5122		0.085		0.015	
w2v	50	0.923		0.508		0.151		0.027	
w2v-sem	10292	0.906		0.519		0.260		0.048	

config	dim	tc	ct	tc	ct	tc	ct	tc	ct
+lsa-50	100	0.9225	0.9214	0.5223	0.5222	0.166	0.195	0.030	0.036
+lsa-100	150	0.9202	0.9207	0.5164	0.5217	0.188	0.202	0.038	0.038
+lsa-250	300	0.9197	0.9165	0.5198	0.5289	0.181	0.246	0.037	0.040
+lsa-500	550	0.9218	0.9053	0.5190	0.5337	0.159	**0.305**	0.030	**0.059**
+pca-50	100	0.9208	0.9101	0.5195	0.5329	0.193	0.242	0.039	0.049
+pca-100	150	0.9207	0.9141	0.5206	**0.5349**	0.178	0.234	0.036	0.047
+pca-250	300	0.9217	0.9146	0.5217	0.5250	0.171	0.237	0.035	0.044
+pca-500	550	0.9223	0.9107	0.5202	0.5254	0.161	0.255	0.032	0.049
+kmeans-50	100	0.9089	0.9257	0.5267	0.4821	0.252	0.018	0.056	0.005
+kmeans-100	150	0.9028	**0.9272**	0.5107	0.4811	0.133	0.000	0.028	0.000
+kmeans-250	300	**0.9272**	**0.9272**	0.4811	0.4811	0.000	0.000	0.000	0.000
+kmeans-500	550	**0.9272**	**0.9272**	0.4811	0.4811	0.000	0.000	0.000	0.000

Table 2: Experimental results on the MultiLing 2015 MSS dataset using 50-dimensional word2vec embeddings. Bold values indicate maxima across rows for that column. Underlined values correspond an improvement over the counterpart configuration (tc versus ct, or x versus x-sem).

config	dim	mi-F		ma-F		Rouge-1		Rouge-2	
gt	N/A	1.000		1.000		0.414		0.132	
prob	N/A	0.871		0.501		0.051		0.009	
BOW	15852	0.9254		0.5131		0.094		0.017	
TF-IDF	15852	0.9260		0.5122		0.085		0.015	
fastext	300	0.923		0.517		0.156		0.029	
fastext-sem	10542	0.919		0.516		0.204		0.043	

config	dim	tc	ct	tc	ct	tc	ct	tc	ct
+lsa-50	350	0.9167	0.9214	0.5231	0.5195	0.206	0.182	0.038	0.032
+lsa-100	400	0.9200	0.9212	0.5196	0.5224	0.171	0.189	0.032	0.036
+lsa-250	550	0.9237	0.9134	0.5221	0.5370	0.145	0.278	0.031	0.053
+lsa-500	800	0.9243	0.9083	0.5201	**0.5373**	0.128	**0.296**	0.025	**0.056**
+pca-50	350	0.9186	0.9145	0.5205	0.5319	0.182	0.234	0.036	0.045
+pca-100	400	0.9208	0.9160	0.5187	0.5369	0.160	0.230	0.037	0.044
+pca-250	550	0.9233	0.9146	0.5210	0.5286	0.189	0.229	0.038	0.045
+pca-500	800	0.9239	0.9096	0.5223	0.5261	0.152	0.255	0.032	0.047
+kmeans-50	350	0.8995	0.9238	0.4928	0.4833	0.071	0.022	0.018	0.006
+kmeans-100	400	0.8903	**0.9272**	0.4897	0.4811	0.071	0.000	0.018	0.000
+kmeans-250	550	**0.9272**	**0.9272**	0.4811	0.4811	0.000	0.000	0.000	0.000
+kmeans-500	800	**0.9272**	**0.9272**	0.4811	0.4811	0.000	0.000	0.000	0.000

Table 3: Experimental results on the MultiLing 2015 MSS dataset using 300-dimensional fasttext embeddings. Bold values indicate maxima across rows for that column. Underlined values correspond an improvement over the counterpart configuration (tc versus ct, or x versus x-sem).

makes these measures less indicative of system performance, compared to Rouge.

- **Does the semantic augmentation process benefit via dimensionality reduction post-processing methods?**

The augmentation process can improve with post-processing methods. This is expected, since the sparse bag-based semantic vectors are bound to contain noise and/or redundant and overlapping information that will affect the learning model further down the summarization pipeline. For both embeddings examined, such configurations improve upon the baseline and achieve the best scores, for all evaluation measures included.

LSA-based transformations achieve top Rouge performance for both embeddings covered, as well as top F1 scores for the fastext embedding, with its frequency-based decomposition appearing to work better than PCA analysis. On the contrary, K-means clustering mostly failed to capture underlying semantic content into meaningful groups, especialy for higher dimensions examined. Additionally, the post-processing transformation methods work best mostly when applied to the concatenated lexical and semantic vectors, rather than transforming the semantic information alone and then conatenating.

Apart from the specific research questions, it is notable that the large class imbalance has to be carefully handled, as – even with the dataset oversampling measures taken – the sentence classifier can converge into degenerate cases, as was the case with the higher dimensional configurations of K-means.

At this point, we note that since our system does not account for selected sentence order, we limit our comparison of each approach to only the gt configuration, rather than the human-authored summaries; even for cases with perfect classification performance, the results are far from optimal (e.g. Rouge 1, Rouge 2 scores of 1.0) since there is no guarantee that sentence order is preserved in the extractive ground truth generation, detailed in 4.1. This introduces an upper bound to performance and prevents meaningful comparison to related work. Instead, this study illustrates the contribution of semantic information to the pipeline, as illustrated above.

As a last note, we compare our results with respect to the unaltered, human-written summaries – i.e. which are not composed of input sentences as per the extractive setting, after reiterate that our preliminary approach does not take into account sentence order or target length. First, the gt extractive ground truth we generated achieves an Rouge-1 and Rouge-2 score of 0.245 and 0.57 respectively, effectively serving as an upper bound for our performance. The best-performing 500-dimensional LSA configuration for word2vec trained embeddings performs at 0.196 and 0.015 for Rouge-1 and Rouge-2, respectively, and 0.191, 0.014 for fasttext. These results fall short of the system performance levels on previous MultiLing community tasks (Conroy et al., 2015), however the goal of this investigation was solely to illustrate the utility of the semantic component; future work (outlined below) plans on addressing this issue and align our results toward related work comparability.

5 Conclusions

In this work, we investigated the contribution of semantically enriching word embedding-based approaches to extractive summarization. Pre-trained embeddings as well as embeddings trained from scratch on the target dataset were utilized. For the semantic channel, frequency-based concept information from Wordnet is extracted, post-processed with a range of feature transformation and clustering methods prior or after concatenation with the lexical embeddings. A wide evaluation was performed on multiple configuration combinations and transformation dimensions, using micro/macro F1 and Rouge-1/Rouge-2 scores. Initial results show semantic such augmentation approaches can introduce considerable benefits to baseline approaches in terms of macro F1, Rouge-1 and Rouge-2 scores, with micro-F1 deemed inadequate for highly imbalanced problems such as the extractive summarization setting examined here. LSA-based decomposition works best out of the variants examined, outperforming PCA and K-means post-processing in terms of Rouge. In the future, more sophisticated transformation methods could be explored, such as encoder-decoder schemes via recurrent neural networks (Hochreiter and Schmidhuber, 1997), dynamically fusing word embeddings into a sentence encoding and eliminating the need for word averaging in sentence-level vector generation. Alternatively, sequence-based classification could be explored in a similar fashion. Moreover, higher transformation dimensions could be covered, given the best configuration examined lied on the highest end of the exmained range (500) and additional semantic resources can be utilized, via the bag-based approach used in this study, or by alternative methods of semantic vector generation (Faruqui et al., 2014). Finally, the natural next step in our work would be the application of our semantic augmentation approach with a sentence ranking and a target length constraint mechanisms, in order to make the results of pipeline fairly comparable to related summarization systems.

References

Abdelkrime Aries, Djamel Eddine Zegour, and Khaled Walid Hidouci. 2015. Allsummarizer system at multiling 2015: Multilingual single and multi-document summarization. In *Proceedings of the 16th Annual Meeting of the Special Interest Group on Discourse and Dialogue*. pages 237–244.

Collin F Baker, Charles J Fillmore, and John B Lowe. 1998. The berkeley framenet project. In *Proceedings of the 17th international conference on Computational linguistics-Volume 1*. Association for Computational Linguistics, pages 86–90.

Kedar Bellare, Anish Das Sarma, Atish Das Sarma, Navneet Loiwal, Vaibhav Mehta, Ganesh Ramakrishnan, and Pushpak Bhattacharyya. 2004. Generic text summarization using wordnet. In *LREC*.

Piotr Bojanowski, Edouard Grave, Armand Joulin, and Tomas Mikolov. 2017. Enriching word vectors with subword information. *Transactions of the Association for Computational Linguistics* 5:135–146.

Kurt Bollacker, Colin Evans, Praveen Paritosh, Tim Sturge, and Jamie Taylor. 2008. Freebase: a collaboratively created graph database for structuring human knowledge. In *Proceedings of the 2008 ACM SIGMOD international conference on Management of data*. AcM, pages 1247–1250.

Peter F Brown, Peter V DeSouza, Robert L Mercer, Vincent J Della Pietra, and Jenifer C Lai. 1992. Class-based n-gram models of natural language. *Comput. Linquistics* 18(1950):467–479. http://www.aclweb.org/anthology/J92-4003.

John M. Conroy, Jeff Kubina, Peter A. Rankel, and Julia S. Yang. 2015. *Multilingual Summarization and Evaluation Using Wikipedia Featured Articles*, chapter Chapter 9, pages 281–336.

CHENGHUA Dang and XINJUN Luo. 2008. Wordnet-based dcument summarization. In *WSEAS International Conference. Proceedings. Mathematics and Computers in Science and Engineering*. World Scientific and Engineering Academy and Society, 7.

Scott Deerwester, Susan T ST Dumais, George W GW Furnas, Thomas K Landauer, and Richard Harshman. 1990. Indexing by latent semantic analysis. *J. Am. Soc. Inf. Sci.* 41(6):391. https://doi.org/10.1002/(SICI)1097-4571(199009)41:6¡391::AID-ASI1¿3.0.CO;2-9.

Zakaria Elberrichi, Abdelattif Rahmoun, and Mohamed Amine Bentaalah. 2008. Using wordnet for text categorization. *International Arab Journal of Information Technology (IAJIT)* 5(1).

Manaal Faruqui, Jesse Dodge, Sujay K. Jauhar, Chris Dyer, Eduard Hovy, and Noah A. Smith. 2014. Retrofitting word vectors to semantic lexicons. *arXiv Prepr. arXiv1411.4166* (i). https://doi.org/10.3115/v1/N15-1184.

Michel Galley, Jonathan Graehl, Kevin Knight, Daniel Marcu, Steve DeNeefe, Wei Wang, and Ignacio Thayer. 2006. Scalable inference and training of context-rich syntactic translation models. In *Proceedings of the 21st International Conference on Computational Linguistics and the 44th annual meeting of the Association for Computational Linguistics*. Association for Computational Linguistics, pages 961–968.

George Giannakopoulos, Jeff Kubina, John Conroy, Josef Steinberger, Benoit Favre, Mijail Kabadjov, Udo Kruschwitz, and Massimo Poesio. 2015. Multiling 2015: multilingual summarization of single and multi-documents, on-line fora, and call-center conversations. In *Proceedings of the 16th Annual Meeting of the Special Interest Group on Discourse and Dialogue*. pages 270–274.

Vishal Gupta and Gurpreet Singh Lehal. 2010. A survey of text summarization extractive techniques. *Journal of emerging technologies in web intelligence* 2(3):258–268.

Zellig S Harris. 1954. Distributional structure. *Word* 10(2-3):146–162.

Trevor Hastie, Robert Tibshirani, Jerome Friedman, and James Franklin. 2005. The elements of statistical learning: data mining, inference and prediction. *The Mathematical Intelligencer* 27(2):83–85.

Sepp Hochreiter and Jurgen Jürgen Schmidhuber. 1997. Long short-term memory. *Neural Comput.* 9(8):1–32. https://doi.org/10.1162/neco.1997.9.8.1735.

Roger A Horn and Charles R Johnson. 2012. *Matrix analysis*. Cambridge university press.

Chihli Hung and Stefan Wermter. 2004. Neural network based document clustering using wordnet ontologies. *International Journal of Hybrid Intelligent Systems* 1(3-4):127–142.

Anjali Ganesh Jivani, Others, and Ganesh Jivani Anjali. 2011. A comparative study of stemming algorithms. *Int. J. Comp. Tech. Appl* 2(6):1930–1938. https://www.researchgate.net/profile/Anjali_Jivani/publication/284038938_A_Comparative_Study_of_Stemming_Algorithms/links

Ian Jolliffe. 2011. Principal component analysis. In *International encyclopedia of statistical science*, Springer, pages 1094–1096.

Armand Joulin, Edouard Grave, Piotr Bojanowski, and Tomas Mikolov. 2016. Bag of tricks for efficient text classification https://arxiv.org/pdf/1607.01759.pdf.

S Katz. 2003. Estimation of probabilities from sparse data for the language model component of a speech recognizer (February):2–4.

Dawn Lawrie, W Bruce Croft, and Arnold Rosenberg. 2001. Finding topic words for hierarchical summarization. In *Proceedings of the 24th annual international ACM SIGIR conference on Research and development in information retrieval*. ACM, pages 349–357.

Quoc Le and Tomas Mikolov. 2014. Distributed representations of sentences and documents. In *International Conference on Machine Learning*. pages 1188–1196.

Yann LeCun, Yoshua Bengio, Geoffrey Hinton, Lecun Y., Bengio Y., and Hinton G. 2015. Deep learning. *Nature* 521(7553):436–444. https://doi.org/10.1038/nature14539.

Lei Li, Yazhao Zhang, Liyuan Mao, Junqi Chi, Moye Chen, and Zuying Huang. 2017. Cist@ clscisumm-17. Multiple features based citation linkage, classification and summarization. In *BIRNDL@ SIGIR (2)*. pages 43–54.

Marina Litvak and Mark Last. 2013. Multilingual single-document summarization with muse. In *Proceedings of the MultiLing 2013 Workshop on Multilingual Multi-document Summarization*. pages 77–81.

Ying Liu, Peter Scheuermann, Xingsen Li, and Xingquan Zhu. 2007. Using wordnet to disambiguate word senses for text classification. In *international conference on computational science*. Springer, pages 781–789.

Elena Lloret and Manuel Palomar. 2009. A gradual combination of features for building automatic summarisation systems. In *International Conference on Text, Speech and Dialogue*. Springer, pages 16–23.

Stuart Lloyd. 1982. Least squares quantization in pcm. *IEEE Trans. Inf. theory* 28(2):129–137.

Trevor N Mansuy and Robert J Hilderman. 2006. Evaluating wordnet features in text classification models. In *FLAIRS Conference*. pages 568–573.

Victoria McCargar. 2004. Statistical approaches to automatic text summarization. *Bulletin of the American Society for Information Science and Technology* 30(4):21–25.

Rada Mihalcea and Paul Tarau. 2004. Textrank: Bringing order into text. In *Proceedings of the 2004 conference on empirical methods in natural language processing*. pages 404–411.

Tomas Mikolov, Kai Chen, Greg Corrado, and Jeffrey Dean. 2013a. Efficient estimation of word representations in vector space. *arXiv preprint arXiv:1301.3781* .

Tomas Mikolov, Ilya Sutskever, Kai Chen, Greg S Corrado, and Jeff Dean. 2013b. Distributed representations of words and phrases and their compositionality. In *Advances in neural information processing systems*. pages 3111–3119.

George A Miller. 1995. Wordnet: a lexical database for english. *Commun. ACM* 38(11):39–41.

Tatsunori Mori. 2002. Information gain ratio as term weight: the case of summarization of ir results. In *COLING 2002: The 19th International Conference on Computational Linguistics*.

Frederic Morin and Yoshua Bengio. 2005. Hierarchical probabilistic neural network language model. *Proc. Tenth Int. Work. Artif. Intell. Stat.* pages 246–252. https://doi.org/10.1109/JCDL.2003.1204852.

Ani Nenkova and Lucy Vanderwende. 2005. The impact of frequency on summarization. *Microsoft Research, Redmond, Washington, Tech. Rep. MSR-TR-2005* 101.

Joel Larocca Neto, Alex A Freitas, and Celso AA Kaestner. 2002. Automatic text summarization using a machine learning approach. In *Brazilian Symposium on Artificial Intelligence*. Springer, pages 205–215.

Alok Ranjan Pal and Diganta Saha. 2014. An approach to automatic text summarization using wordnet. In *2014 IEEE International Advance Computing Conference (IACC)*. IEEE, pages 1169–1173.

Jeffrey Pennington, Richard Socher, and Christopher Manning. 2014. Glove: Global vectors for word representation. In *Proceedings of the 2014 conference on empirical methods in natural language processing (EMNLP)*. pages 1532–1543.

Matt Post and Shane Bergsma. 2013. Explicit and implicit syntactic features for text classification. In *Proceedings of the 51st Annual Meeting of the Association for Computational Linguistics (Volume 2: Short Papers)*. volume 2, pages 866–872.

D Radev, H Jing, and M Budzikowska. 2000. Centroid-based summarization of multiple documents: Clustering, sentence extraction, and evaluation. In *Proceedings of the ANLP/NAACL-2000 Workshop on Summarization*.

Radim Rehurek and Petr Sojka. 2011. Gensim—statistical semantics in python. *statistical semantics; gensim; Python; LDA; SVD* .

M Rodriguez, J Hidalgo, and B Agudo. 2000. Using wordnet to complement training information in text categorization. In *Proceedings of 2nd International Conference on Recent Advances in Natural Language Processing II: Selected Papers from RANLP*. volume 97, pages 353–364.

Gerard Salton and Christopher Buckley. 1988. Term-weighting approaches in automatic text retrieval. *Inf. Process. Manag.* 24(5):513–523.

Gerard Salton, Anita Wong, and Chung-Shu Yang. 1975. A vector space model for automatic indexing. *Commun. ACM* 18(11):613–620.

Sam Scott and Stan Matwin. 1998. Text classification using wordnet hypernyms. *Usage of WordNet in Natural Language Processing Systems* .

Sam Scott and Stan Matwin. 1999. Feature engineering for text classification. *ICML* 99:379–388. https://pdfs.semanticscholar.org/6e51/8946c59c8c5d005054af319783b3eba128a9.pdf.

Marta Vicente, Oscar Alcón, and Elena Lloret. 2015. The university of alicante at multiling 2015: approach, results and further insights. In *Proceedings of the 16th Annual Meeting of the Special Interest Group on Discourse and Dialogue*. pages 250–259.

Yiming Yang. 1997. A comparative study on feature selection in text categorization http://www.surdeanu.info/mihai/teaching/ista555-spring15/readings/yang97comparative.pdf.

Jaya Kumar Yogan, Ong Sing Goh, Basiron Halizah, Hea Choon Ngo, and C Puspalata. 2016. A review on automatic text summarization approaches. *Journal of Computer Science* 12(4):178–190.

HEvAS: Headline Evaluation and Analysis System

Marina Litvak, Natalia Vanetik, Itzhak Eretz Kdosha
Software Engineering Department,
Shamoon College of Engineering,
Beer Sheva, Israel
`{marinal,natalyav,itzhaer}@ac.sce.ac.il`

Abstract

Automatic headline generation is a sub-task of one-line summarization with many reported applications. Evaluation of systems generating headlines is a very challenging and undeveloped area. We introduce the Headline Evaluation and Analysis System (HEvAS) that performs automatic evaluation of systems in terms of a quality of the generated headlines. HEvAS provides two types of metrics—one which measures the informativeness of a headline, and another that measures its readability. The results of evaluation can be compared to the results of baseline methods which are implemented in HEvAS. The system also performs the statistical analysis of the evaluation results and provides different visualization charts. This paper describes all evaluation metrics, baselines, analysis, and architecture, utilized by our system.

1 Introduction

A headline of a document can be defined as a short sentence that gives a reader a general idea about the main contents of the story it entitles. There have been many reported practical applications for headline generation (Colmenares et al., 2015) or related tasks. Automatic evaluation of automatically generated headlines is a highly important task, where a candidate headline is assessed with respect to (1) readability (i.e. whether the headline is easy to understand), and (2) relevance (i.e. whether the headline reflects the main topic of an article). Building unbiased metrics that manage to make objective evaluations of these properties has been proved to be a difficult task. Some of the related work resort to human-assisted evalua-

tion (Zajic et al., 2002), which is undoubtedly expensive and time-consuming. Therefore, most of works rely on the existing tools for automatic evaluation such as ROUGE (Shen et al., 2016; Hayashi and Yanagimoto, 2018). The main assumption being that because the metrics work well for standard summaries, the same applicable to short summaries and headlines, as a private case. However, authors of (Colmenares et al., 2015) provide statistical evidence that this statement does not necessarily hold. We suspect that the main reason is that a summary needs to convey the content of a document while a headline should introduce, but not describe, the main subject of a document. Moreover, even very short summaries usually include at least two full sentences while headlines do not. Despite that discovery, not many attempts to develop special metrics for the headline evaluation were made. Two new metrics—an adaptation of a ROUGE metric, and a metric for comparing headlines on a conceptual level using Latent Semantic Indexing (LSI) —were introduced in (Colmenares et al., 2015)

2 Related Work

This section surveys the metrics used recently in literature for a headline evaluation task and approaches we use for the introduced metrics as part of HEvAS. For the rest of this paper the terms "reference headline" and "candidate headline" will be used to address the human-generated and the automatically generated headlines, respectively.

2.1 ROUGE metrics

ROUGE metrics (Lin, 2004) are widely used for evaluation of summaries, aiming to identify content overlap—in terms of word n-grams—between gold-standard (reference) summaries and the evaluated (system) summary.
ROUGE-N

Proceedings of the Multiling 2019 Workshop, co-located with the RANLP 2019 conference, pages 73–80
Varna, Bulgaria, September 6, 2019.
http://doi.org/10.26615/978-954-452-058-8_010

This recall-oriented metric measures the number of N-grams in the reference headline that are also present in a candidate headline. It is defined as: $\frac{|n\text{-}grams(R) \cap n\text{-}grams(C)|}{|n\text{-}grams(R)|}$, where R refers to the reference headline, C to the candidate headline, and the function $n\text{-}grams$ returns the set of contiguous N-grams of words in a text. In our system we use the ROUGE-N metric with $N = 1$ and $N = 2$.

ROUGE-SU

One of the problems of using the ROUGE-N metric (with $N > 1$) is that requesting headlines to share contiguous N-grams might be a very strong condition. This is even more problematic when taking into account that headlines are comprised, on average, of 8-10 tokens. This metric combines ROUGE-1 with a relaxed version of ROUGE-2 that takes into account non-contiguous (skip) bigrams. For example, *"President Trump said"* will produce three skip bigrams: *"President Trump,"* *"President said,"* and *"Trump said."* Let's denote a function that returns all unigrams of the headline H as $1\text{-}grams(H)$, and a function that returns its skip-bigrams as $s2\text{-}grams(H)$. Then formally, $ROUGE\text{-}SU(R, C)$ is defined as follows: $\frac{|su(R) \cap su(C)|}{|su(R)|}$, where $su(H) = 1\text{-}grams(H) \cup s2\text{-}grams(H)$. By allowing gaps between bigrams, this metric detects similarities among phrases that differ by adjectives, or small changes.

ROUGE-WSU

The main problem of ROUGE-SU is that it gives the same importance to all skip-bigrams extracted from a phrase. For instance, suppose that the following phrases were compared: H_1 : *"x B C x x"*, H_2 : *"B y y y C"*, H_3 : *"z z B z C"*. The only skip-bigram they all have in common is *"B-C,"* and ROUGE-SU gives us the same similarity score between the three of them. Authors of (Colmenares et al., 2015) proposed to weight the skip-bigrams with respect to their average skip-distance. Formally, it must be calculated as: $\dfrac{\sum\limits_{(a,b) \in su(R) \cap su(C)} \frac{2}{dist_R(a,b) + dist_C(a,b)}}{\sum\limits_{(a,b) \in su(R)} \frac{1}{dist_R(a,b)}}$ where function $dist_H(a, b)$ returns the skip distance between words *"a"* and *"b"* in headline H. For unigrams, the function returns 1. This measure produces different scores for H_2 and H_3 in our example. Namely, ROUGE-WSU(H_1, H_3) > ROUGE-WSU(H_1, H_2).

2.2 Averaged Kullback–Leibler divergence

The Kullback–Leibler divergence is a measure of how two probability distributions are different. It is widely used for measuring the similarity between texts, as the distance between the probability distributions of their words. However, the KL-divergence is not symmetric and cannot be used as a distance metric. Therefore, the averaged KL-divergence is used instead, which is defined as follows (Huang, 2008): $D_{AvgKL}(\vec{t_a} \| \vec{t_b}) = \sum_{t=1}^{m} (\pi_1 \times D(w_{t,a} \| w_t) + \pi_2 \times D(w_{t,b} \| w_t))$, where $\vec{t_a}$ is a vector representation of a text (document or headline in our case) a, $w_{t,a}$ is a weight[1] of term t in a text a, $\pi_1 = \frac{w_{t,a}}{w_{t,a} + w_{t,b}}$, $\pi_2 = \frac{w_{t,b}}{w_{t,a} + w_{t,b}}$, and $w_t = \pi_1 \times w_{t,a} + \pi_2 \times w_{t,b}$.

2.3 Latent Semantic Indexing

The ROUGE and KL-Divergence metrics relate two headlines only on the basis of word co-occurrences, i.e., they compare headlines at a very low syntactic level (token matching). We also need other metrics that are able to detect abstract concepts in the text and useful for both comparing headlines at a semantic level and measuring of a headline's coverage of a document topics. For this end, authors of (Colmenares et al., 2015) decided to use Latent Semantic Indexing (LSI) to extract latent concepts from a corpus and represent documents as vectors in this abstract space. The similarity was then computed by means of angular distances. The exact steps that were performed in (Colmenares et al., 2015), are as follows: (1) a document-TF-IDF matrix M is built; (2) Singular Value Decomposition (SVD) is performed on M resulting in matrices USV^T; (3) the eigenvalues in matrix S are analyzed and filtered; (4) the transformation matrix VS^{-1} is calculated, which enables the translation of TF-IDF document vectors to vectors in latent space; (5) after computing latent space vectors for both the headline and the entire document, their cosine similarity is calculated.

2.4 Topic Modeling

Topic model is a type of statistical model for discovering the abstract "topics" that occur in a collection of documents. Latent Dirichlet allocation (LDA) (Blei et al., 2003; Blei, 2012) allows documents to have a mixture of topics. LDA uses a

---

[1] The *tf-idf* (term frequency inverse document frequency) weighting scheme or a basic *tf* (term frequency) can be used.

generative probabilistic approach for discovering the abstract topics, (i.e., clusters of semantically coherent documents). In particular, we define a *word* as the basic discrete unit of any arbitrary text, which can be represented as an item w indexed by a vocabulary $\{1, 2, \cdots, |V|\}$. A *document* is then a sequence of N words denoted by $\mathbf{w} = (w_1, w_2, \cdots, w_N)$. Finally, we define a *corpus* of M documents as $\mathbf{D} = \{\mathbf{w}_1, \mathbf{w}_2, \cdots, \mathbf{w}_M\}$. LDA finds a probabilistic model of a corpus that not only assigns high probability to members of the corpus, but also assigns high probability to other similar documents (Blei et al., 2003).

2.5 Word Embeddings

Word embeddings is another approach for building a semantically-enriched text representation, which provides a good basis for comparison between two texts at the semantic level. Word embeddings represent words as dense high-dimension vectors. These dense vectors model semantic similarity, *i.e.*, semantically similar words should be represented by similar dense representations while words with no semantic similarity should have different vectors. Typically, vectors are compared using a metric such as cosine similarity, euclidean distance, or the earth movers distance (Kusner et al., 2015). Two well-known methods to acquire such dense vector representations are word2vec (Mikolov et al., 2013) and GloVe (Pennington et al., 2014). Both methods are based on the concept of distributional semantics, which exploits the assumption that similar words should occur in similar surrounding context.

2.6 Readability Assessment

Generation of readable headlines is not an easy task. Therefore, evaluation of headlines must include readability measurements. Most works in this area are based on a key observation that vocabulary used in a text mainly determines its readability. It is hypothesized that the use of common-frequently occurring in a language words makes texts easier to understand. Because it was observed that frequent words are usually short, word length was used to approximate the readability instead of frequency in many works (Kincaid et al., 1975; Gunning, 1952; Mc Laughlin, 1969; Coleman and Liau, 1975). According to (DuBay, 2004), more than 200 formulae for measuring readability exist. A survey of readability assessment methods can be found in (Collins-

Thompson, 2014). However, most of readability metrics are designed for larger texts and not applicable for a single headline.

3 The HEvAS System

HEvaS aims at evaluation of systems for headline generation in terms of multiple metrics, both from informativeness and readability perspectives. The results can be analyzed and visualized. This section describes all metrics and system settings that can be specified by the end user.

3.1 Informativeness Metrics in HEvAS

In this paper, we propose 12 informativeness metrics for headline evaluation, some are novel and some are adopted from the literature, which comprise the base for the introduced evaluation framework.

ROUGE metrics
ROUGE-1,2,SU, and WSU metrics are used for measuring similarity between a candidate and reference headlines.

Averaged KL-Divergence
We used averaged KL-Divergence for measuring both (1) *similarity* between the generated headline and its reference title, and (2) the headline's *coverage* of important keywords representing a document, as its similarity to the document.

TM-based metrics
We apply LDA topic modeling[2] on the input documents. The following outputs of the LDA algorithm, normalized and treated as probabilities, are relevant to our studies: (1) Topic versus word dictionary, which gives the word w distributions $P(w|P_i)$ for each topic P_i; (2) Inferred topic distributions for each document d in the studied corpus, namely the probability $P(P_i|d)$ (θ_i parameter of the LDA model) that a certain document d belongs to a topic P_i; (3) Importance of every topic in a document d, $P(d|P_i)$.

Given the LDA's output, we compute vector representations in a topics space for headlines (candidate and reference) and their documents, as follows: Each headline H and each document d are represented by a vector over K topics, where each topic P_i is assigned a weight computed as a normalized sum of word-in-document-topic importance $P(w|P_i)P(P_i|d)P(d|P_i)$ over all words w in P_i. In order to evaluate a headline, two metrics are calculated: (a) the headline's *coverage* of im-

---

[2]Mallet tool (Graham et al., 2012) was used.

portant topics representing a document, as a cosine similarity between the headline and the document vectors; and (b) *similarity* to the reference headlines, as a cosine similarity between the headline and the references vectors.

LSI-based metrics

We adopt the LSI-DS metric from (Colmenares et al., 2015) for measuring a headline's *coverage* of latent topics of its document. In addition, we extend it to the *similarity* between system and reference headlines by computing latent space vectors for both types of headlines and measuring a cosine similarity between their vectors. Also, our system allows a user to decide how to filter (if at all) the number of eigenvalues: by absolute number, by ratio, or by filtering out the values below a specified threshold.

Word Embedding-based metrics

This metric is based on Google's word2vec model, in which every word from the English vocabulary is assigned with a 300-dimension vector. We use the average vector (as a standard) to represent multiple words. For example, a headline is represented by an average vector calculated from representations of all its words. Similarity between two representations is measured by cosine similarity, which may imply similarity in content. As such, also two types of metrics are supported: (1) the headline's *coverage* of important topics representing a document, as a cosine similarity between the headline and the document vectors; (2) *similarity* to the reference headlines.

3.2 Readability Metrics in HEvAS

Currently, HEvAS contains the following five metrics: (1) **Proper noun ratio (PNR)**. It is hypothesized that higher PNR indicates higher readability (Smith et al., 2012), because proper nouns contribute to a text disambiguation. (2) **Noun ratio (NR)**. NR is used to capture the proportion of nouns present in the text. The text with lower proportion of nouns is considered to be easier to read (Hancke et al., 2012). (3) **Pronoun ratio (PR)**. PR is a linguistic measure indicating the level of semantic ambiguity that can arise while searching for the concept that a pronoun represents.(Štajner et al., 2012) A text with lower PR is considered more readable. (4) **Gunning fog index**. In linguistics, the Gunning fog index (Gunning, 1952) is a readability test for English writing. We use the following formula: $Fog = 0.4 *$

$(\#words + 8 * \frac{\#complex\ words}{\#words})$, where $\#words$ is the headline length. (5) **Average word length (AWL)**. The AWL reflects the ratio of long words used in a text. It was proven that the use of long words makes a text more difficult to understand for dyslexics. (Rello et al., 2013)

3.3 Baselines

For comparative evaluations and a possibility to get impression about relative performance of the evaluated systems, five baselines are implemented in HEvAS: (1) *First* compiles a headline from nine first words; (2) *Random* extracts nine first words from a random sentence; (3) *TF-IDF* selects nine top-rated words ranked by their $tf - idf$ scores; (4) *WTextRank* generates a headline from nine words extracted by the TextRank algorithm (Mihalcea and Tarau, 2004) for the keyword extraction; (5) *STextRank* extracts nine first words from the top-ranked sentence by the TextRank approach for extractive summarization.

3.4 Statistical analysis and visualization

To determine whether the difference between system scores is statistically significant, the statistical significance test must be applied. HEvaS performs Tukey test (Jones and Tukey, 2000) if the results are normally distributed, and Wilcoxon test (Bergmann et al., 2000) otherwise.

To visualize the results of evaluation, the system generates the following plots for all evaluated systems and chosen metrics: (1) Bar plot (with or without confidence intervals); (2) Box plot (five number summary); (3) Scatter graph for visualizing cross-correlation between metrics.

3.5 HEvAS Implementation

The system is implemented in Java as a standalone application and is available for download[3] in a .zip archive[4]. The demo video is provided.[5] HEvAS provides the following options to the end user: (1) **Provide input files**. The documents, their gold titles, and the generated headlines must be provided as an input for every evaluation run. The documents with their (reference) headlines must be provided as one (xml-like formatted) file;

---

[3]The current version of HEvAS supports only Windows OS.

[4]https://drive.google.com/file/d/
1-7Z--XMfmlbzjzyKlFOLfCKDEvAm0eNq/view?
usp=sharing

[5]https://drive.google.com/open?id=
1BoaV9CUoZHJqMfAC1pQRXsSCka4-3jQO

and all headlines generated by one system are also must be organized in one file.[6] All files are required to be UTF-8 plain texts in English. (2) **Specify output files**. All results, including the summarizing statistics and charts (specified by the user), are saved to the file system. The folder for those files location must be provided by the user. (3) **Choose metrics**. The user can specify which category (informativeness or readability) of metrics and which metrics from each category she wants to apply in the evaluation process. Some metrics are also must be configured with additional settings. For example, LSI metrics require additional settings for optional filtering latent eigenvalues; (4) **Choose charts**. The user can specify which charts she wants to use for the visualization of the evaluation results. (5) **Choose baselines**. The user may specify which baselines to use for the comparative evaluations. Figure 1 depicts the flowchart of the HEvAS system, with its main modules.

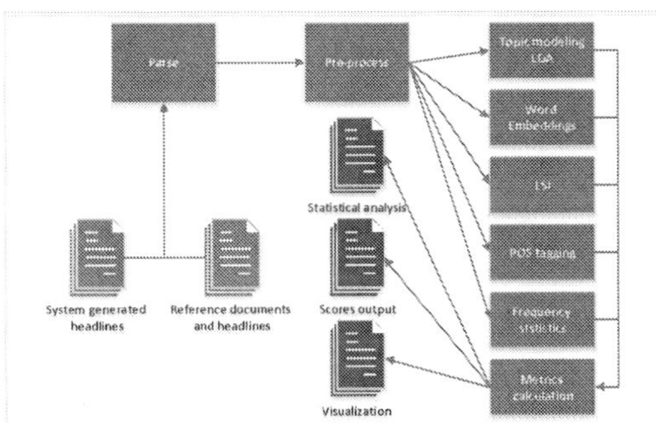

Figure 1: HEvAS data flow

Once evaluation is finished, its results are visualized at the system's interface and written to the file system. For every headline generation system the output file (in csv format) is generated, where columns stand for chosen metrics and rows stand for the input documents. Also, one summarizing csv file is generated where all systems can be ranked by their avg metric scores. One single score for each system is calculated as an average for every metric. Additionally, an average score over all metrics is calculated for every system; this is possible because all of the metrics are $[0, 1]$-normalized. Figure 2 shows an example of

final average scores of competing systems as generated by HEvAS. Figure 3 shows an example of

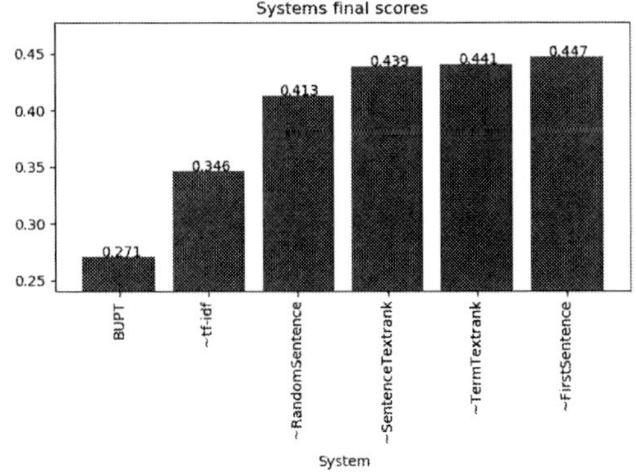

Figure 2: Average scores over all metrics for all systems

metric average scores for the first sentence taken as a headline, generated by HEvAS.

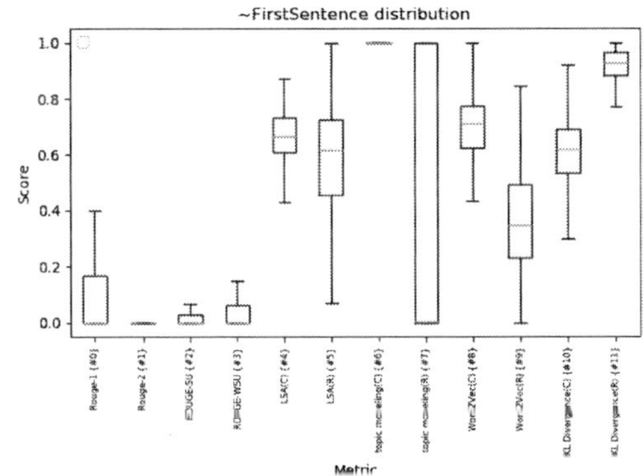

Figure 3: All average metric scores for the first sentence system

4 Experiments

We performed experiments on a small dataset composed of 50 wikinews articles written in English[7], where each document is accompanied by a reference (gold standard) headline. The dataset is

---

[6]The examples of such files are provided with the software.

[7]Despite the experiments were performed on English documents only, some metrics of HEvAS are applicable to other languages. Extension of all HEvAS metrics to multilingual environment is a part of our future work.

System/Metric	R-1	R-2	R-SU	R-WSU	LSA-C	LSA-S	TM-C	TM-S	WE-C	WE-S	KL-C	KL-S
Random	0.046	0.000	0.011	0.018	0.869	0.721	0.783	0.586	0.693	0.445	0.593	0.954
TF-IDF	0.008	0.000	0.002	0.003	0.980	0.731	0.338	0.470	0.650	0.390	0.578	0.951
First	0.408	0.177	0.176	0.236	0.892	0.828	0.925	0.691	0.734	0.735	0.664	0.959
STextRank	0.191	0.066	0.061	0.096	0.904	0.781	0.794	0.608	0.732	0.579	0.692	0.932
WTextRank	0.263	0.009	0.082	0.114	0.857	0.768	0.923	0.663	0.735	0.613	0.719	0.906

Table 1: Mean scores of informativeness metrics.

System/Metric	Fog	NR	PNR	PR	AWL
Random	0.740	0.471	0.004	0.004	6.318
TF-IDF	0.786	0.511	0.000	0.000	6.853
First	0.410	0.396	0.006	0.017	5.154
STextRank	0.446	0.357	0.005	0.020	4.987
WTextRank	0.863	0.584	0.002	0.000	6.040

Table 2: Mean scores of readability metrics.

publicly available.[8] Table 1 contains mean scores per each informativeness metric (with default settings) for all five baselines (see Section 3.3). Each metric, except ROUGE, was applied for a coverage (denoted by C suffix) and a similarity (denoted by S suffix) scenarios. Table 2 contains the results of readability metrics for all baselines.

The results of a correlation analysis[9] between informativeness metrics demonstrate a high correlation between all ROUGE metrics and between ROUGE metrics and Word Embedding similarity-based metric (WE-S). Figure 4 shows correlation achieved for ROUGE-1 and ROUGE-SU metrics. However, a low correlation was obtained between

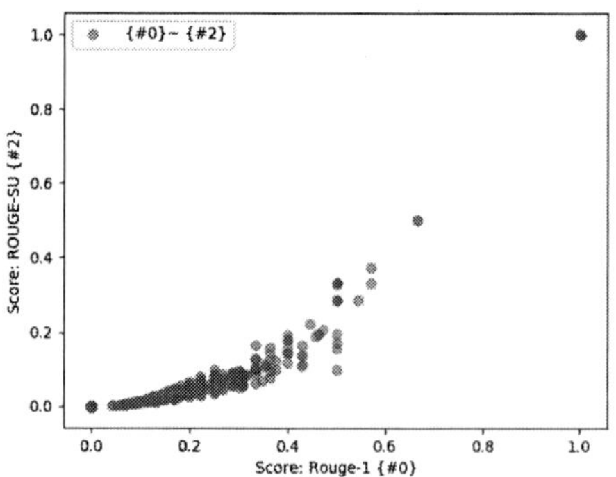

Figure 4: Correlation between ROUGE-1 and ROUGE-SU metrics

all other metrics. Also, coverage metrics usually

do not correlate with the similarity metrics of the same type (an exception—correlation 0.6—was observed in a case of TM-based metrics). There are no correlated readability metrics. The lowest negative correlation (-0.5) was found between AWL and Gunning Fog Index and between PNR and NR. Detailed correlation scores between different metrics achieved for our dataset are given in Table 3.

5 Conclusions and future work

In this paper we presented a working system named HEvAS for automated headline evaluation. The HEvAS system provides a user with 12 metrics, where some of them are novel, which measure headline quality in terms of informativeness—topics coverage and closeness to the human-generated headlines. Also, HEvAS provides five readability metrics, which measure how understandable the headlines. The system provides an output which enables to rank different systems by their scores. Most HEvAS metrics are adaptable to multiple languages. However, some metrics require an additional effort, such as training word vectors or applying a POS tagger on a corpus in a target language. Our future work includes the following tasks: (1) extension of our system with more metrics, especially metrics measuring the grammatical correctness of the generated headlines; (2) adaptation of HEvAS to multiple languages (in progress); and (3) measuring the correlation of automatic metrics with the human judgements (in progress).

[8]https://drive.google.com/file/d/
1JHKH4-49UwbKdx7MIXJaLZSd444AUKFc/view?
usp=sharing

[9]Performed for the *First* baseline using Pearson correlation.

	R-1	R-2	R-SU	R-WSU	LSA-C	LSA-S	TM-C	TM-S	WE-C	WE-S	KL-C	KL-S
R-1	-	0.74	0.99	0.99	-0.30	0.43	0.24	0.19	0.07	0.85	0.34	0.09
R-2	0.745	-	0.76	0.78	-0.16	0.35	0.07	0.07	-0.09	0.66	0.11	0.21
R-SU	0.991	0.76	-	1.00	-0.32	0.41	0.23	0.18	0.03	0.84	0.32	0.12
R-WSU	0.995	0.78	1.00	-	-0.31	0.42	0.23	0.18	0.05	0.85	0.32	0.11
LSA-C	-0.305	-0.16	-0.32	-0.31	-	0.28	-0.17	-0.11	-0.14	-0.21	-0.21	0.01
LSA-S	0.427	0.35	0.41	0.42	0.28	-	0.26	0.24	-0.08	0.44	-0.03	0.05
TM-C	0.237	0.07	0.23	0.23	-0.17	0.26	-	0.60	0.28	0.38	0.18	-0.03
TM-S	0.187	0.07	0.18	0.18	-0.11	0.24	0.60	-	0.11	0.28	0.06	-0.05
WE-C	0.075	-0.09	0.03	0.05	-0.14	-0.08	0.28	0.11	-	0.26	0.44	-0.39
WE-S	0.849	0.66	0.84	0.85	-0.21	0.44	0.38	0.28	0.26	-	0.29	0.00
KL-C	0.345	0.11	0.32	0.32	-0.21	-0.03	0.18	0.06	0.44	0.29	-	-0.34
KL-S	0.088	0.21	0.12	0.11	0.01	0.05	-0.03	-0.05	-0.39	0.00	-0.34	-

Table 3: Metric correlation scores.

References

Reinhard Bergmann, John Ludbrook, and Will PJM Spooren. 2000. Different outcomes of the wilcoxon-mannwhitney test from different statistics packages. *The American Statistician* 54(1):72–77.

D M Blei. 2012. Probabilistic topic models. *Communications of the ACM* 55(4):77–84.

D. M. Blei, A. Y. Ng, and M. I. Jordan. 2003. Latent dirichlet allocation. *Journal of Machine Learning Research* 3:993–1022.

Meri Coleman and Ta Lin Liau. 1975. A computer readability formula designed for machine scoring. *Journal of Applied Psychology* 60(2):283.

Kevyn Collins-Thompson. 2014. Computational assessment of text readability: A survey of current and future research. *ITL-International Journal of Applied Linguistics* 165(2):97–135.

Carlos A Colmenares, Marina Litvak, Amin Mantrach, and Fabrizio Silvestri. 2015. Heads: Headline generation as sequence prediction using an abstract feature-rich space. In *Proceedings of the 2015 Conference of the NAACL: HLT*. pages 133–142.

William H DuBay. 2004. The principles of readability. *Online Submission* .

Shawn Graham, Scott Weingart, and Ian Milligan. 2012. Getting started with topic modeling and mallet. Technical report, The Editorial Board of the Programming Historian.

Robert Gunning. 1952. The technique of clear writing.
.

Julia Hancke, Sowmya Vajjala, and Detmar Meurers. 2012. Readability classification for german using lexical, syntactic, and morphological features. *Proceedings of COLING 2012* pages 1063–1080.

Yuko Hayashi and Hidekazu Yanagimoto. 2018. Headline generation with recurrent neural network. In *New Trends in E-service and Smart Computing*, Springer, pages 81–96.

Anna Huang. 2008. Similarity measures for text document clustering. In *sixth New Zealand computer science research student conference (NZCSRSC2008)*. pages 49–56.

Lyle V Jones and John W Tukey. 2000. A sensible formulation of the significance test. *Psychological methods* 5(4):411.

J Peter Kincaid, Robert P Fishburne Jr, Richard L Rogers, and Brad S Chissom. 1975. Derivation of new readability formulas (automated readability index, fog count and flesch reading ease formula) for navy enlisted personnel .

M. J. Kusner, Y. Sun, N. I. Kolkin, and K. Q. Weinberger. 2015. From word embeddings to document distances. In *ICML*.

Chin-Yew Lin. 2004. Rouge: A package for automatic evaluation of summaries. In *Proceedings of the Text Summarization Branches Out workshop*.

G Harry Mc Laughlin. 1969. Smog grading-a new readability formula. *Journal of reading* 12(8):639–646.

Rada Mihalcea and Paul Tarau. 2004. Textrank: Bringing order into text. In *Proceedings of the EMNLP*.

Tomas Mikolov, Kai Chen, Greg Corrado, and Jeffrey Dean. 2013. Efficient estimation of word representations in vector space. *arXiv preprint arXiv:1301.3781* .

Jeffrey Pennington, Richard Socher, and Christopher D Manning. 2014. Glove: Global vectors for word representation. In *EMNLP*. ACL, volume 14, pages 1532–1543.

Luz Rello, Ricardo Baeza-Yates, Laura Dempere-Marco, and Horacio Saggion. 2013. Frequent words improve readability and short words improve understandability for people with dyslexia. In *IFIP Conference on Human-Computer Interaction*. Springer, pages 203–219.

Shiqi Shen, Yu Zhao, Zhiyuan Liu, Maosong Sun, et al. 2016. Neural headline generation with sentence-wise optimization. *arXiv preprint arXiv:1604.01904* .

Christian Smith, Henrik Danielsson, and Arne Jönsson. 2012. A good space: Lexical predictors in vector space evaluation. In *LREC 2012*. Citeseer, pages 2530–2535.

Sanja Štajner, Richard Evans, Constantin Orasan, and
Ruslan Mitkov. 2012. What can readability measures really tell us about text complexity. In *Proceedings of workshop on natural language processing for improving textual accessibility*. Citeseer,
pages 14–22.

David Zajic, Bonnie Dorr, and Richard Schwartz. 2002.
Automatic headline generation for newspaper sto-
ries. In *Workshop on Automatic Summarization*.

Author Index